SUSTAINABLE
JEWELLERY

Principles and Processes for Creating an Ethical Brand

JOSE LUIS FETTOLINI

promopress

SUSTAINABLE JEWELLERY
Principles and Processes for Creating an Ethical Jewellery Brand

Copyright © 2018 Promopress

Texts, selection of contents and edition: Jose Luis Fettolini
English translation and revision: Tom Corkett
Layout design: Jose Luis Fettolini
Layout revision and adaptation: Antonio G. Tomé
Cover design: Mireia Casanovas Soley
Cover and back cover images: photographs selected from the
interior of the book
Image correction: Toni Rovira
Editorial coordination: Montse Borràs

Introduction by Dr. Greg Valerio

ISBN: 978-84-16851-20-1
D.L.: B 8914-2018

Promopress is a brand of:
Promotora de Prensa Internacional S.A.
C/ Ausiàs Marc 124
08013 Barcelona, Spain
Phone: 0034 93 245 14 64
Fax: 0034 93 265 48 83
email: info@promopress.es
www.promopresseditions.com
Facebook: Promopress Editions

Printed in Malaysia

FOREWORD

THE TRUTH ABOUT BEAUTY
by Greg Valerio

There can be no doubt, jewellery is an enigmatic product. I can think of no other purchase that is so emotionally poignant. I guess this is the great paradox that has kept me in the jewellery game all these years. Its character and inconstancies continue to capture my attention on a daily basis.

As an ethical jeweller of over 20 years I have always approached jewellery from the bottom up. Not the perfectly rounded bottoms of the air brushed models used by the jewellery fashionistas to seduce customers into the false narrative that jewellery equals better sex. I am an iconoclast of the luxury jewellery convention, where the true bottoms in our profession are bent double in muddy pools processing small volumes of gold, diamond or gemstone, eked out of marginal ground in the forgotten corners of our glorious world.

It is this moral disconnect with the truth of jewellery, that our great profession is so scared of, and it is into this disconnect that every intentional ethical jeweller and consumer must be brave enough to step into. It takes great courage to be ethical in life as well as jewellery.

It is true, over my twenty years in the trade, I have witnessed time and again, some of the cruelest, degrading, exploitative and ecologically abusive practices that humanity can conjure. All of this degradation of humanities nobility and creations beauty done in the name of precious metals and minerals and the subsequent jewels we create from these materials.

This is the complicated context that ethical jewellers unashamedly get involved in. Unscrambling the omelette is not easy. Re-addressing the trade disparities in gold is fraught with danger, as I found out in Kenya in 2013 when I was chased out of the country under threats of violence by the local illegal traders. I am a fair trade ethical jeweller and proud of it. Being intentionally ethical does not devalue my jewellery, as Cartier once told me it would do theirs.

The value of jewellery is not in the colour of the box, it is in the efficacy of the source. Ethical jewellery claims are founded upon two basic principles, transparency and traceability. Without these two pillars in place, talk of ethical jewellery (ηθικός ethikos, meaning what actions are right or wrong in particular circumstances) is meaningless. If luxury jewellery brands are not prepared to dignify their sources with consumer disclosure, the consumers should not dignify that brand with a purchase of product.

However this is just the beginning of the ethical jewellery story. Jewellery is a natural product, a treasure from the earth that brings joy and meaning. A gift, a talisman, a treasure from the deep, which speaks of value and worth. Measuring this value is important and jewellery should always represent these truthful values. The value of craftsmanship, the genius of design, the beauty of natural gemstones, the richness of gold. To authentically value the human hand from which the jewel emerged and the integrity of the eco system that gave birth to it, is as important as the design of the jewel itself. Jewellery is worn to beautify, there is no beauty in exploitation.

Writing a foreword for this book is a privilege. This is an important book, because it heralds another step in re-writing the story of jewellery and inspiring the consumer with quality information that will tell the truth about the beauty, the dignity and the wonder of the sources of all jewellery. It will tell the story of the challenges, the sweat, the injustices and the exploitation that occurs because we love to buy jewellery. But most importantly it will inform and guide the lovers of jewellery to ask the right questions when they buy a jewel so their purchase leaves a positive legacy in the communities from where the materials originate.

Dr. Greg Valerio MBE
Jeweller & Activist
www.valeriojewellery.com - Online Store
www.gregvalerio.com - Blog

PREFACE

The concept of sustainability is in the ascendant. We can see that different sectors, including the fashion world, are developing sustainability strategies to offer lower-impact products in order to counteract the effects of an economic model that is based on constant growth. These sectors are also carrying out the important task of conducting campaigns to educate and raise awareness among their target public about responsible consumption. This has created a great flow of information for both consumers and designers.

But when we are talking about jewellery, do we really know what lies behind each piece?

The truth is that the jewellery industry is capable of having a much more negative impact than other sectors do. That impact affects both the environment and social conditions, and it can be found throughout the supply chain. However, because of the secrecy and lack of transparency that characterize this sector and the profession, it is often difficult to know the extent of that impact. This makes it difficult to do business in a sustainable way.

The lack of information available has meant that many designers are not aware of the impact that their activities have, or of the alternatives or solutions that can be implemented at the start of the creative process in order to create jewellery according to sustainable criteria.

To counteract these shortcomings, this book offers the information that many jewellery designers have been waiting to receive. With the help of collaborations with a range of organizations and firms, this book brings together a long list of suppliers and certifications for sustainable raw materials so that a business model that is more respectful of the environment and social ethics can be established. Through an in-depth examination of the different key links that comprise the supply chain, it is possible to ascertain the damaging impact that jewellery production can bring about. Without this knowledge, it would be difficult to implement alternatives that are truly efficient and sustainable.

Through case studies, examples and interviews with designers and representatives of international firms that have taken up the challenge of creating ethical and responsible jewellery, this book aims to serve as inspiration for any designer who wishes to run a jewellery firm in a sustainable way.

It is my hope that reading this work will inspire in you the desire to throw yourself into this new challenge.

Jose Luis Fettolini

1
WHAT IS SUSTAINABILITY?

1.1 | The Gold Core collection by Tejen
Earrings and pendant made from 18k Fairmined gold.
Photo: Andrew Yee

Introduction

It is not unusual for people to talk about sustainability today, and it is a fairly widespread concept. However, understanding its requirements demands an in-depth study of current business models and of the urgent changes that these require.

Our consumption habits tend to involve positive expectations about society's growth and development, but at the same time they are based on an irresponsible business model that does not consider the collateral damage that it may cause. This feeds a rampant consumerism that causes us to lose sight of the true value of things.

At present, we accept the serious situation that we face, but this exploitation of resources and destruction of the environment is often understood as something remote that we have no responsibility over. We know that we are its cause, but it is hard for us to accept that we are also harmed. We view nature as an entity separated from us and not as the habitat that our survival depends on.

The concept of sustainability

Concern with sustainability is certainly not new. The concept first appeared in 1987 in the Brundtland Report (also known as *Our Common Future*), which was produced for the UN by former Norwegian prime minister Gro Harlem Brundtland. Its findings warned of the environmental problems caused by economic development and globalization.

But what many people do not know is that the international community has been worried about this subject for many years. One example is the theory that Thomas Malthus set out in his book *An Essay on the Principle of Population*, a work published back in 1798. In it, Malthus explains that populations tend to grow faster than resources do. The reality is that, more than two hundred years on from Malthus, we can see that this theory was on the right track: we find ourselves on an overcrowded planet, where we consume natural resources faster than the planet can regenerate them.

Today's critical environmental situation was predicted more than 200 years ago.

Economic and social evolution

Society's evolution toward economic growth during the twentieth century has led us to a point where the consequences are beginning to be serious. The problem with this type of development is that it is only focused in one direction. It does not take into consideration the other factors involved such as environmental and social aspects.

We can sense that the socioeconomic model under which we live has many cracks in it and that it requires changes directed toward making a society that is more equitable and respectful toward the environment. This has awakened a collective consciousness that is shared far beyond a small group of environmentalists. A growing sector of society, aware of the scope of this problem, has decided to act to offer global solutions.

Under these circumstances, and with regard to the design world, this awareness requires us to ask many questions that will help us to find appropriate solutions. The starting point is to understand the complexity of the issue so that the concept of sustainability no longer has an ambiguous meaning.

Sustainable values

Fortunately, this has brought about an awareness that is easily perceived in almost everything around us. It is a sociological trend founded upon values that make possible a sustainability that takes a global perspective and considers environmental protection, social development and economic growth that creates wealth in a way that is fair to all.

ENVIRONMENTAL PROTECTION

ECONOMIC GROWTH

SUSTAINABILITY

SOCIAL DEVELOPMENT

Responsible consumption

This collective awakening has made us talk more and more about the need for ecological and ethical solutions to a real problem that affects all of us. This in turn has aroused the conscience of many consumers who have developed an empathy toward their environment. They are concerned not only about their own interests but also about the common good. They are consumers with scruples who do not just seek pleasure and benefits for themselves and who wish to consume more responsibly by taking into account industrial activities' direct effect on the environment, excessive resource use, human rights violations, labour exploitation, gender inequality, the use of child labour and the abuse of animals.

The conscious consumer has unleashed new needs within the market by demanding products that comply with demonstrable ethical values.

New needs

What are these requirements? First of all, the truth about the activities carried out is one of the fundamental pillars. Consumers require guarantees about the products that they consume and about the ethical policies of each company. This means that many firms and designers have been compelled to rethink the way in which they set up their supply chain. They have had to incorporate innovative ideas that provide solutions within a new business model based on ethics and respect for the environment, and also and above all on the honesty expected by the consumer.

We must not forget that, directly or indirectly, we are all part of the system, which means that we are all consumers. As a result, this new demand is also being met by the awareness of the many designers, companies and organizations that see the problem and the need for change.

The personal convictions and the efforts taken by many professionals in different sectors to follow a different path to the conventional one allow us to enjoy products that are much more sustainable, ethical and respectful and that give back value and true meaning to the objects we use every day, whether as accessories, clothing or food.

Mining, which is linked to the jewellery sector, is a destructive, polluting and cruel industry.

Obviously, any activity carried out by human beings will always have consequences, and the impact or footprint left on the environment can be higher or lower depending on the nature of the industry in question. Even if jewellery making is carried out by hand or in limited production runs, its characteristics and the raw materials used make it an activity that is directly related to mining, one of the most damaging industries for the planet.

As we will see later, environmental pollution and human rights violations are being questioned, and alternatives that control and reduce the cruelty of the industry's procedures are emerging.

The picture in other sectors

Many sectors are implementing improvements related to sustainable practices, a trend that is increasing due to the new demand. Sectors such as fashion, food and the automotive industry are clear examples of this. The paradox is that the sectors or industries that have caused the greatest adverse impact, and that continue to do so, are the ones that are simultaneously responding with alternatives that involve greater respect for the environment.

However, it must be borne in mind that these alternative forms of supply and demand represent a very small percentage relative to the bulk of all consumer products. It is necessary to continue educating and informing the consumer, since many bad practices are the result of complete ignorance about the subject.

Food

The industry that has undergone the most remarkable transformation in recent years is the food sector. After the rise in recent decades of fast food and the abandonment of traditional cooking due to new sociological circumstances, an awareness of how we feed ourselves has come about and taken on a fundamental role. This is reflected in the proliferation of businesses that were created out of the need for and possibility of better food.

Demand for organic products is on the increase, and these can even be found in conventional supermarkets in many countries.

1.2 | Organic Food

More and more people are deciding to change their habits to incorporate healthier and cleaner food. Within this change, demand for locally grown products and support for small farmers represent a new consumption model.

Photo: Condesign / pixabay.com

Fashion

The fashion industry has also gained a reputation for having a highly unethical production model. Big brands have been hit on numerous occasions by scandals related to child labour and the deplorable factory conditions in the developing countries in which their employees work.

In the 1990s, this industry suffered heavy criticism for its use of animal products. Negative campaigns spearheaded by PETA, an international animal rights organization, spread across the world and had a powerful impact that reached as far as the end consumer.

But there continue to be serious failings in this industry's practices, from the environmental damage that cotton monocultures produce to garment manufacturing processes that make highly excessive use of resources such as water. Moreover, it continues to produce pollution, and employees still suffer as a result of its almost nonexistent labour ethics. The aim is obviously to be able to offer new collections and clothing increasingly quickly and to reduce costs as much as possible so that the consumer can buy at a lower price.

1.3 | Handbag by Mayya Saliba
Mayya Saliba has longstanding experience in the field of sustainable fashion, and she focuses on the circular economy. Her company Design & Sustainability provides support and consulting services to the fashion industry.
To create this clutch, she used Piñatex vegetable fibre, a raw material extracted from pineapple plant through an organic process.

Photo: Roland Kunos

1.4 | Adidas footwear

The sportswear firm Adidas, in collaboration with Parley for the Oceans, has created a line of clothing and footwear whose raw materials are plastics recovered from the ocean.
Its big play to reach a mass audience is a new shoe called *Ultra Boost Uncaged Adidas x Parley*, which is made out of 95% recycled plastic from the ocean and the remaining 5% from polyester.
www.parley.tv

Photo: © 2006, adidas AG.

In the long term, it is easy to sense that this business model does not have a very bright future, since it only leads to generating waste at breakneck speed. However, at the same time as the fashion industry is being challenged, alternatives and solutions are being offered under the concept of "slow fashion." Nowadays, a large number of designers and firms are backing fashion based on sustainable and transparent activities in order to develop a form of fair trade that takes into account animal rights and respect for the environment and that places quality above quantity.

But one positive aspect of the fashion sector that is lacking in the jewellery world is the extensive sharing of information and raising of awareness with consumers regarding unethical industry practices that harm the ecosystem and social rights. Every year, countless documentaries, activities and campaigns report from within the abuse that is taking place. The consumer must understand that the industry is not the only cause of the problem, since if we are aware of what is happening, we all shoulder the responsibility of choosing the clothes that we buy.

The automotive sector

The automotive sector's bid for sustainability is based on reducing consumption of nonrenewable resources such as fuels and on offering alternatives such as electric motors, which greatly reduce pollution from CO_2.

The interesting detail here is that these new technologies are not just being used in experimental or practical vehicles. Luxury brands such as BMW, Porsche and Tesla are developing high-performance hybrid and electric vehicles, which suggests that there is real market demand.

1.5

1.5 | BMW i3

The i3 by Germany's BMW is a 100% electric vehicle that emits zero emissions. It has a range of 300 km, and it has up to 170 hp.

Photo © BMW AG, Munich (Germany)

1.6 | Tesla Model S

The American company Tesla is revolutionizing the market for 100% electric vehicles through a philosophy based on sustainability. Its quest for innovation is also focused on creating and developing domestic solar panels and batteries to provide greater energy savings.

Photo: © Tesla Motors, Inc.

1.6

Developing awareness

The jewellery industry is divided into different segments that are based on style, materials, price range and consumer profile, among other factors. In a nutshell, its various strands can be classified as high jewellery, designer jewellery, commercial or fashion jewellery, and contemporary or artistic jewellery. Of course, the markets for each of these types of jewellery are very different, but it is also the case that the basis and processes for turning an idea into a physical piece are very similar. Regardless of the production volume, all jewellery stems from an idea that gives way to a design process in which the concepts to be developed are put forward.

Within this design process, materials are selected, particular trends are studied, and plans are made as to the mode of production, whether this takes an artisanal or more industrialized form. Once production has been completed, the goal of any firm or designer is to bring the piece of jewellery or the collection to a point of sale where it will find a consumer interested in it.

We can either conduct this process just as we have learned to do it until now, or we can include a series of questions that make us reflect on the impact that we can have, since until we ascertain and understand what the issues are, we will not be able to find solutions. But facing real problems in a practical, decisive and resolute way always entails a personal decision for each jeweller or designer. Sustainability is a path that we have to undertake with convictions of our own based on personal values and concerns.

IDEAS > CONCEPTS > DESIGN > MATERIALS

The first step

Undertaking sustainable practices in the jewellery sector is a process that should always begin with a series of key questions that make us reconsider what we are doing.

It is highly likely that the simple fact of asking these questions means that doubt is already being cast on our current situation. We sense that there is something that we are not doing well and that we do not have all the necessary information on the materials that we are working with. This is a disconcerting situation that we want to respond to as soon as possible. However, as I have already said, all this starts with a general question:

What to ask oneself

Am I aware of the environmental and ethical impact produced by my activity?
This question encompasses other, more specific questions:

What are the conditions under which my suppliers work?
What guarantees do I have about the raw materials that I use and about their origins?
Does my business fall within the criteria for fair trade?
Do I really want my jewellery pieces to be linked to the suffering of others?
What should I do to provide ethical and environmental solutions?
Is my jewellery brand or firm ready to contribute to a better future?

PRODUCTION > RETAIL

Looking for answers

Once we have responded to all of these questions, we will be aware of the need to contribute to social well-being. We will have to stop thinking at the individual level and understand that global problems also affect us, even if they do so indirectly or over time.

Contributing to making this well-being possible requires an in-depth knowledge of the difficulties, shortages and challenges that many people face, and it also demands an understanding of our ecosystem's fragility and of the fact that any action undertaken will always have an impact, whether positive or negative.

Accordingly, by thinking beyond the narrow scope of designers, craftspeople or jewellers, we will be able to take creativity to a higher level to find solutions, phasing out traditional blueprints and clearing the way for new tools that contribute to creating a more ethical and equitable world.

1.7 | Collection of rings by Fluid

After a few years spent working as a jewellery designer, Caelen Ellis, founder of the Canadian firm Fluid Jewellery, experienced a change in his professional and personal life—an awakening of consciousness that forced him to ask himself a simple question: What is the impact of my individual actions? Shortly after, the concept of "mindful luxe" became the fundamental principle that he applied to his designer jewellery. In its jewellery pieces, the firm uses Fairmined gold and silver, recycled metals and conflict-free diamonds.

Photo: Alex Lauzon and Mantis Gangné

Building the future

To build a better future, it is not enough for us just to understand the different problems. We also have to act decisively and resolutely. But how do we do this?

In the following chapters, apart from detailing the actual conflicts in the jewellery industry, I intend to demonstrate that many designers and jewellery firms have already started to head down an ethical and responsible path, which suggests that an alternative to the status quo is possible. Through different interviews and case studies, we will learn how this challenge arose for each designer and what the solutions and alternatives needed to create a model of sustainable development have been.

However, at this point I can state that the key is to analyse our environment carefully, thinking about the consequences of each of our activities and working out what alternatives there may be. It is not a question of creating a piece of jewellery and, once it has been made, thinking about how it could become more sustainable, since all these new concepts must be applied throughout and not at the end of a creative process.

1.8 | Praise of Shadows: earrings by Ute Decker made from sustainable gold

Ute Decker, a German artist and jewellery maker based in London, is an international pioneer in using sustainable metals under the Fairtrade mark. Her convictions have brought her to the head of a movement that advocates the ethical practices that are so highly necessary in this industry.
These earrings, made from 18k Fairtrade ethical gold, were selected by architect Zaha Hadid as a standout piece at the Goldsmiths' Fair in London in 2014.

Photo: Ute Decker

Lia Terni

1.9

1.10

Brazilian designer Lia Terni was the first creator of jewellery in Spain to use sustainable metal certifications, first with the Eco Gold project and later with Fairmined.

Her involvement in fashion opened her eyes to how cruel and unethical this industry can be. Knowing about this reality led her to consider a brand project that was sustainable from its beginnings. Her minimalist style, which was inspired by architecture, has become established within the wedding jewellery sector.

1.9 | Lia Terni
Photo: Rocío Ramos

1.10 | Ring by Lia Terni
Ring made from Fairmined gold and quartz.
Photo: Rocío Ramos

What were your reasons for adopting sustainability?

I have been working in the field of fashion and design for more than fifteen years, in addition to having developed my own brand. During this time, I have witnessed a huge number of unethical or unsustainable practices, mainly during collaborations with large groups. I was there for the boom in offshoring and "fast fashion."

It seemed to me that being a small company provided me with a huge opportunity to sow seeds of greater fairness in all senses. I wasn't happy about being part of a machine that was highly destructive to the environment and communities. That was how it all started: with my stopping for a moment and thinking about everything in the processes that could improve.

1.11 | Lia Terni headband

Headband made with Fairmined gold and 1.2 carat diamonds. Earrings made from Fairmined gold and chalcedony.

Photo: Rocío Ramos

How do you connect Lia Terni's values with its customers?

For me, there is no better feeling than to have customers who come to the brand because they are looking for a jewellery piece that has value not only through its materials or design but also through the whole story behind it (no use of chemicals in the extraction, no child labour, no destruction of the environment). Minimizing the footprint that we leave on our environment is no longer an option. It is a necessity.

When I launched the project and began to explain the impacts of jewellery making on communities and the environment to customers, I sensed a certain discomfort—almost guilt—on their part about not having had this information before. Today, there is much more information, and millennials seem to have already incorporated this concept into their thinking to a greater extent, which I think is very interesting for new generations of jewellers.

Lia Terni has been using ecological gold for several years. Can you describe what your experience with Green Gold was like?

Lia Terni was the first company in Spain to have its purchasing of raw materials extracted in a fair manner to be certified. At that time in Spain, there was no information about the existence of these processes, even with regard to Fairtrade. Heading down this road has been an important experience in my career, and I have experienced the great satisfaction of being able to do things in a fairer way.

Lia Terni

Your main focus is wedding jewellery. How do you see the sustainable value of jewellery pieces outside of this niche?

The value of sustainability should be in each and every thing. Without a doubt, getting to that point will be a process. I believe that the desire to "do things right" gets bigger following key life moments such as a wedding or the birth of a baby. My personal experience is that there is a greater chance that people are open to acknowledging sustainability at such moments. I have some new projects that will make this concept reach a larger group of people.

How do you see Lia Terni's future? What other goals based on sustainable practices do you want to bring in?

Lia Terni's future is to continue to do its bit for best practices in the jewellery world. This means extending this concept to all aspects of the business, from how workshop waste is handled to how to do packaging.

1.14

What advice would you give to new designers who want to make their collections ethical and responsible when it comes to the environment?

The more of us there are, the better things will be for the environment and communities. We will spread the message's reach in the world together. The road will be a very hard one if we go it alone. I invite everyone to collaborate with each other and to always have an open and inclusive outlook.

1.13 | | Lia Terni wedding rings set
Wedding rings made from Fairmined gold.
Photo: Rocío Ramos

1.14 | Lia Terni comb
Contemporary interpretation of a traditional Spanish comb made from Fairmined gold; earrings made from Fairmined gold.
Photo: Rocío Ramos

1.12 | Lia Terni bridal set
Headband, earrings and ring made of Fairmined gold and chalcedony.
Photo: Rocío Ramos

Adidas by Parley
www.adidas.com/us/parley

BMW AG, Munich
www.bmw.com

Fluid Jewellery
www.fluid-jewellery.myshopify.com

Goldsmiths Fair of London
www.goldsmithsfair.co.uk

Lia Terni
www.liaterni.com

Mayya Saliba
www.mayyasaliba.com

Piñatex by Ananas Anam
www.ananas-anam.com/pinatex/

Tesla Motors
www.tesla.com

Ute Decker
www.utedecker.com

Zaha Hadid
www.zaha-hadid.com

2
REALITIES AND NEEDS

2.1 | Wedding ring by Diamond Foundry

Wedding ring by Diamond Foundry made from 18k gold and diamonds produced in a laboratory.

Photo: Diamond Foundry Inc.

2.2

To understand the jewellery industry's need for sustainable practices, the main thing that needs to be known is the realities of the sector and its problems. The harmful impact generated by this industry rests on two key points: social repercussions and environmental effects. Knowing about these two factors allows us to be able to see the problem so as to implement solutions in the areas of design, regulations, production and resource management.

The high price of the raw materials that are most commonly used in jewellery making often exerts a great pressure on the countries and communities that these materials come from, fomenting a black market in which there is rampant speculation and corruption and in which the social and working conditions of the most disadvantaged people involved in this business are at best secondary or tertiary concerns. Exploitation, torture, child labour and human rights violations are the harmful practices that we might encounter today.

Social conditions

The jewellery industry has always to a certain degree sealed itself off from the end consumer, and it has offered only very limited information about the origins of its raw materials and its practices in this area. However, in 2006, everyone became alert to some truly terrible things as a result of Edward Zwick's film Blood Diamond. The film recounts the brutal reality of the diamond trade in Sierra Leone, a country plagued for more than 9 years during the 1990s by a civil war in which trafficking and exploitation related to diamonds played a big role. Thousands of people became slaves in the diamond mines as their lives hung by a thread. Death, murder and human rights violations are what lie behind so-called blood diamonds. What is a dream for a few is a nightmare for many.

But Sierra Leone is not the only country where there have been armed conflicts and human rights abuses as a result of diamond-related exploitation and trafficking. Other African countries such as Angola and the Democratic Republic of the Congo are clear examples of how the wealth that lies under the ground has become the direct cause of misery for some countries' inhabitants.

A symbol of love, or a symbol of exploitation and human rights violations?

2.3

2.2 | Deforested landscape, Colombia
Illegal mining causes uncontrolled deforestation in many Latin American, African and Asian countries.
Photo: Mauricio Vélez

2.3 | Diamonds
Photo: Soo Hee Kim / Shutterstock.com

Many documentaries have portrayed the crude business hidden behind diamond exploitation in different countries where labour rights are nonexistent today. This picture produces a major contradiction when we talk about diamonds, a symbol of eternal love. For many disadvantaged groups who cannot find another way to survive, diamonds have in fact become a symbol of exploitation.

The widespread sharing of such information has allowed a large number of consumers to develop an awareness of the origins of the jewellery that they buy and to demand ethical products that respect human rights.

It is not only diamonds that have been tainted by these bad practices. The majority of precious stones are also obtained under the shadow of exploitation, in appalling working conditions. For example, in Myanmar's ruby industry, a network of exploitation and distribution controlled by the army puts more than 50,000 people to work in one of the world's biggest mines under completely illegal pay and safety conditions.

2.4 | Tanzanian gold miner

The gold mining industry in Tanzania has a long tradition. Many Tanzanian young people, some of them minors, are lured to the gold mines in the hopes of a better life and end up working in illegal mines, in highly insecure and hazardous conditions that include the manipulation of toxic substances such as mercury.

Photo: africa924 / Shutterstock.com

Mining related to the extraction of precious metals also has links to unethical practices from both environmental and social perspectives. In countries with substantial gold and silver deposits in Latin America—for example, Colombia—artisanal and small-scale mining is connected to many social problems such as child labour, terrible working conditions and gender inequality.

To all this we must add that the situation is even worse when groups working outside the law gain control of illegal mining to finance their objectives, brutally destroying the areas where they operate and abusing the most vulnerable and disadvantaged populations.
Johanna Mejía (founder of Amalena).

Such injustices and ethical failings are not limited to the extraction of raw materials. Due to the offshoring encouraged by various free trade agreements, many companies have moved their production to countries where wages are lower and labour regulations and conditions are less strict. They have done so with the aim of increasing profits and without contemplating the damage that these countries' inhabitants may have suffered as a result.

These practices cannot be associated with the large companies in the sector alone, since production in Southeast Asian countries or in China, where jewellery making is more widespread, is already within the grasp of almost anyone, including small companies and firms. Thanks to the Internet and to the ease of international movement nowadays, it is possible to create connections between companies from different countries, regardless of their size. Manufacturers' demand for large-scale production has fallen, meaning that capital investment is much lower, attracting small and medium-sized businesses that carry out offshored production.

Many of their workers are unskilled and lacking in economic resources or even at risk of social exclusion, and this allows entrepreneurs and factory owners to turn to exploitative employment practices with an extremely high risk of accidents and with salaries that do not cover even the most basic needs. Shifts go on for 14 hours, regardless of the weather conditions; there are no rest days; and it is not unusual for the daily wage to be just a dollar. In most cases, the local community itself has to provide the little food that it can for the miners, a large percentage of whom are very young and, because of their size, can pass through very small holes and chip away for hours to advance through the rock.

The mark left on nature

The jewellery industry is not only linked to social problems. It produces among the most severe impacts on the environment that our planet suffers. An analysis of its supply chain reveals its effects in terms of both the extraction of raw materials and the manufacturing of pieces of jewellery.

The first major environmental impact can be found in large-scale mining, whether this is for metals or gems.

This type of controlled and industrialized mining is usually done in the open or in underground mines.

Even when this form of mining involves major safety assurances, it should not be forgotten that its impact on the ecosystem is considerable due to deforestation and land encroachment that change the Earth's morphology irreversibly. Since these mining companies belong to large lobbies, in the case of the extraction of metals such as gold, it is very difficult to know if any type of infringement related to toxic spills is being committed during the process of removing impurities, which uses chemical elements such as cyanide. Despite this lack of information, it is estimated that this industry causes 10% of the planet's mercury pollution.

2.5 | Diamond mining
Surface diamond mining in Sakha Yakutia, northern Russia.

Photo: Alice Nerr / Shutterstock.com

Industrialized mining accounts for 80% of the world's gold extraction. The output goes to the finance, jewellery, technology and surgery instruments.

The remaining 20% is extracted through Artisanal and Small-Scale Gold Mining (ASGM), which generally involves underground or placer mining. In most cases, this type of extraction takes place illegally, as the majority of national- and international-level mining regulations focus on large- and medium-scale activities and overlook the real needs of artisanal and small-scale mining. This means that work of this kind is usually undertaken under very precarious conditions.

One of the major environmental issues is the methods used for processing gold to obtain it in pure form. To separate gold from other sediments, toxic elements such as mercury are used in a totally irresponsible manner that has brought with it a huge increase in water pollution.

A large part of that mercury is poured into soils and rivers, but it also evaporates due to the practices that illegal mining operations use to separate the amalgam. The harmful elements then return to the ground through rainfall, and they are scattered for miles around.

The mercury ultimately becomes methylmercury, or organic mercury, which can be assimilated by living beings, creating a cycle of pollution that starts with algae when they assimilate the methylmercury. Microscopic animals that feed on the algae are eaten by small fish, which in turn are eaten by larger fish that accumulate increasingly harmful particles. These fish end up in the human food chain, causing major health problems. Some of the most serious effects here are to the nervous system, and they can take the form of genetic malformations in newborns.

2.6 | Illegal placer mining
Illegal gold mining in the River Cauca, Colombia.
Photo: Julio Sánchez, courtesy of El País Colombia

All this amounts to a clear attack on the environment. At the same time, however, ethical and social factors come into play, since public health is also affected, not only with regard to the miners and their families, who are in direct contact with toxic substances without any protection, but also in terms of the communities close to the mines and anyone who eats the contaminated fish. The movement of fish shoals across oceans can generate alarming levels of pollution on a large scale.

It should be noted that the mining sector is the world's main consumer of mercury.

This also makes it the main cause of pollution, due to its improper use of the chemical. It is responsible for 40% of emissions of this poisonous ingredient, totalling 727 tons of discharge each year.

Artisanal and small-scale mining also has another type of harmful impact in the regions in which it operates. With the goal of aiding the search for gold, it is common for rivers to be rechannelled to generate small reservoirs of water on which search efforts are focused. This entails deforestation that damages the area's biodiversity almost irreversibly.

2.7

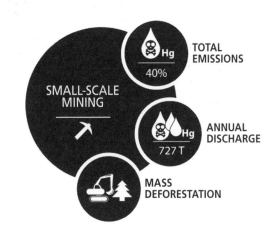

SMALL-SCALE MINING

Hg
40%
TOTAL EMISSIONS

Hg
727 T
ANNUAL DISCHARGE

MASS DEFORESTATION

Ethical practices and social rights

Once we have seen the problems linked to social and labour rights, we will appreciate that the path to providing effective solutions is a long one. Many international organizations, including the UN, have attempted to put certain programmes into practice to ensure that gems and metals from conflict areas do not enter the global market.

In order to control the exploitation of diamonds, in 2003 the Kimberley Process was established. This certification system aims to exclude countries that are at war from entering the diamond market.

However, this measure does not guarantee that the conditions and salaries of the people involved are fair, even if a country is not in a state of war or political instability. This certification initiative has been criticized for its inefficiency. In 2013, the international NGO Global Witness, which participated in the creation of the Kimberley Process, withdrew from the initiative on the ground that it was not halting the laundering of blood diamonds.

2.7 | Artisanal mining in Chocó, Colombia

Illegal miners handling trays with mercury with the aim of creating an amalgam with the gold that they have collected throughout the day.

Photo: Mauricio Vélez

2.8 | Fair mining

An artisanal, small-scale miner in San Roque, Colombia, working in a mine with Fairmined certification.

Photo: ARM

2.8

But thanks to other alternatives and initiatives such as that proposed by Rapaport, it is possible to achieve greater traceability for gems and precious metals, thereby improving social conditions for certain communities in the form of fair wages and labour rights.

The Alliance for Responsible Mining (ARM) seeks to offer wholly decent conditions to the people involved in the artisanal and small-scale mining of precious metals. It is introducing safety standards and promoting economic incentives for best practices, thus ensuring welfare and growth for the communities concerned. Mining operations must comply with certain standards related to labour regulations, and these also ensure traceability.

2.9 | Rings by VK Design

Wedding rings made from Fairmined gold in compliance with the Alliance for Responsible Mining's standards.

Photo: Valerie Kasinskas

Sustainability as a core value

If we wish to bring sustainable practices into a jewellery project as a core value, we must take into account both the environmental impact of our activity and the social and ethical conditions of everyone involved in making the jewellery in question.

We can see that both elements are sufficiently vulnerable for it to be easy to violate the ethical principles that we seek to defend.

A jewellery firm that backs sustainable values must develop these in two areas: the environment and social ethics.

When it comes to environmental aspects, we must focus our attention on both the raw materials and the jewellery manufacturing process. Noble metals such as gold and silver can be environmentally friendly and extracted in a traditional way with nonpolluting substances. Recycling must also be kept in mind for metals or other materials when creating new jewellery. The gems used in environmentally friendly jewellery must be completely natural and not have undergone any kind of atomic modification to improve, modify or intensify their colour. The use of other materials such as cotton or leather must be analysed in order to understand what their harmful impact is and how it can be reduced. Manufacturing should be controlled in terms of reducing and treating the pollutants that are usually used.

Environmental factors

- Low-impact raw materials
- No use of pollutants
- Untreated gems
- Recycled materials
- Analysis of the use of other materials
- Respect for the environment

Ethical and social factors

- Fair trade
- Labour rights
- Gender equality
- Risk reduction
- Economic development
- Social solutions

Ethics-related aspects take into account the social impact produced. The involve looking out for the rights of all workers involved, ensuring gender equality and eliminating exploitation and hazardous conditions that workers may be subjected to. There are also fair-trade practices, which back the development of certain communities to achieve favourable conditions and well-being or projects designed to favour certain disadvantaged groups.

2.10 | Full Circle Talisman bracelet and pendant by Article 22

Article 22 makes its jewellery with aluminium recycled from scrap produced during war, and it uses local labour in Laos, providing fair economic development and offering solutions to the needs of these communities.

Photo: Article 22

Solutions and challenges

As we have seen up to this point, sustainable jewellery goes a step further in all the aspects mentioned above. First of all, it envisages a product that has a lower impact on the environment, and it must back fair trade and social solutions for the common good.

These practices must be applied in the various activities that a company, firm or designer needs to undertake to carry out its functions. This includes design, production, sales strategies, logistics and packaging for distribution.

2.11 | Wedding ring by Nanini made from Fairmined gold and silver

Designer Nina Strategier founded jewellery firm Nanini in 2006 based on a clear commitment to the environment. Accordingly, the raw materials used in manufacturing its jewellery are Fairmined certified.

Photo: Nina Strategier

2.12 | Glasses pendant by Nehcaa, manufactured using ecological silver, with pink gold plating and onyx

Luz Rodríguez and Frank Baeumchen, founders of the firm Nehcaa, design their jewellery based on sustainability above all.
Under the Fairmined certification, they use ecological silver in all of their pieces.

Photo: Celia Mondéjar Domínguez

Applying sustainable practices to a jewellery project seems complicated at first, because we can see that many areas will be affected if we undertake our activities in a conventional manner. However, as we will see later, what is needed is to go step by step in developing a strategy that is viable and that does not seek to resolve all of these problems at the same time. We must not forget that we will encounter certain obstacles, since we are going to paddle upstream in doing things differently to the established way. We will require greater knowledge and greater involvement to protect our ethical principles and commitment.

2.13 | Engagement rings by Jaume Labro

Jaume Labro is a jewellery firm that specializes in Mokume-gane. It backs progressive initiatives at the social and environmental levels. With the sale of each piece, funds are allocated to different associations and organizations that promote school education in certain African countries, mitigate deforestation activities and regenerate the oceans, among other things.

Photo: Jaume Labro

2.14 | GreenPop Project

GreenPop is an NGO dedicated to planting trees through urban greening and reforestation projects, raising awareness about the environment and getting people involved through festivals and workshops throughout southern Africa.

Photo: Johnny Miller

Once sustainability has been brought into a jewellery project, it becomes one of the designer or firm's essential values and is just a starting point—a philosophy with some very clear principles on how things should be done. The idea is not to achieve a few objectives related to sustainability because improvements can always be made and creative and innovative solutions can also be contributed, at the same time as we continually seek the involvement of customers who demand responsible products. We need to share and promote these values by creating a jewellery firm that is also intelligent and that thinks about the future rather than about short-term profits with immediate results.

2.15 | Fiore Della Notte earrings by Anna Loucah

In collaboration with Jersey Pearl. Anna Loucah created a limited-series collection called Fiore Della Notte. The goal was to only use sustainable raw materials. The pieces are made with recycled 18k blackened gold supplied by Hoover & Strong, with spinel and rubies that are ethically sourced thanks to Ruby Fair, and CarbonNeutral® ayoka pearls from Jersey Pearl.

Photo: © Anna Loucah

New market demand

When it comes to sustainable products, it is clear that there is a new demand in the market that continues to grow. This is due to the extra information that consumers have received owing to a trend that is based on ecological values and social ethics. This new perception had led consumers to wonder about who has made the jewellery that they wish to buy, and where the materials with which it has been manufactured come from.

These new conscious consumers are looking for a unique product and for its value to be more than just economic. Knowledge and sensitivity are part of that search, which leads them to get to know first hand the person who designed and produced their jewellery piece. Social and environmental impacts are also part of consumers' concerns, and they are increasingly well informed thanks to different media outlets and to a growing global awareness.

2.16 | Craftspeople from the firm Soko
Soko works with craftspeople in Kenya to manufacture its jewellery.
Photo: Neil Thomas

A new concept of luxury is offering products that, far from being anonymously mass produced, come with clear information on the people who made them.

2.17 - 2.18 | Bracelets, ring and necklace by Soko

Manufactured by craftspeople in Kenya using recycled brass and cow horn from food-industry leftovers.

Photo: Praise Santos

Generally, it is very difficult for small-scale craftspeople in developing countries to gain access to global markets, and so they find themselves trapped in microeconomies, which limits their growth and development to a few sources of low income due to the different intermediaries involved.

Soko uses a clear and transparent supply chain, and it collaborates with craftspeople in Kenya who are offered entrepreneurial opportunities and the chance to take their local crafts further through the use of new technologies.

These craftspeople and entrepreneurs have terminals and smart phones that give them direct access to Soko's global chain of customers in order to sell their products, and they make 25% higher profits compared to other craftspeople.

They also make an ethical commitment to working with local and recycled raw materials such as brass or cow horn, a by-product from the food industry, which artisans buy ethically from nomadic tribes in Kenya and Uganda.

2.19

2.19 | Bracelet by Soko
Manufactured by artisans in Kenya using recycled brass.
Photo: Jana Cruder

2.20 | Wedding rings by María Goti
María Goti is a designer who works wholeheartedly to offer complete transparency about the origin of the metals and gems that she uses. But it was also her customers who began to demand conflict-free diamonds and ecological metals due to the concern that they felt about being implicated in unethical practices.
Photo: María Goti

2.20

Business opportunities

It is a fact that sustainability is generating new business opportunities for trade focused on the future. The inclusion of emotional values in a product such as respecting and conserving nature or unconditionally supporting human rights is an undeniable incentive.

A segment of the jewellery industry that has undergone big change in this respect is the wedding sector, despite the fact that this is a traditional part of the industry that at first sight would seem unable to evolve much further.

Engagement and wedding rings have always symbolized eternal love due in part to the qualities of the materials such as gold and diamonds that they use. Consumers who discover the reality that hides behind each jewellery piece are finding it increasingly intolerable to accept that the emblem of their love also involves suffering, death, child exploitation and destruction of the environment.

The path to innovation

Contradictory though it may seem, sustainability is closely linked to innovation. Fleeing from a conventional and established system that has not taken into account environmental or ethical and social impacts is not an easy task, as going back to the beginning to do things differently would paralyse all our development. For this reason, we have to think about the solutions that can be adapted to our collective reality. We must implement new business models and innovate to devise different production techniques, while also considering different social activities that will meet the needs of the many individuals or groups involved.

An example of this is Daan Roosegaarde's sophisticated and technology-based Smog Free Project. Concerned about the high pollution suffered by capitals such as Beijing, Roosegaarde decided to develop this ambitious project to eliminate the fog caused by pollution and thus create spaces and parks free of toxic air.

Ionic-charge filtration towers purify the air pollution within a diameter of 40 to 70 metres, and they store pollution particles as a black powder, pushing out fresh and clean air into the environment.

The big idea and a by-product of this project is a ring made with a central cubic form that contains the black powder, which is mainly soot from coal. The cube symbolizes a cubic kilometre of air that the filtration towers have cleaned.

Studio Roosegaarde has also considered the idea of launching a limited-edition ring for which carbon particles subjected to great pressure can be transformed into diamonds.

2.21 | Smog Free Project
Ionic-charge filtration towers.
Photo: Studio Roosegaarde

2.22-2.23 | | Smog Free ring by Studio Roosegaarde
This ring contains a cubic millimetre of coal soot that is equivalent to having cleaned 1 km^3 of contaminated air.
Photo: Studio Roosegaarde

Arabel Lebrusan

In 2010, Arabel Lebrusan, a Spaniard based in London, created a firm of her own that places great importance on ethical standards and uses environmentally friendly materials produced in decent working conditions. Her main pieces are made by hand in craft workshops along the Vía de la Plata, Spain.

2.24 | Arabel Lebrusan

Photo: Cat Lane

2.25 | Engagement rings with precious stones by Arabel Lebrusan

Photo: Cat Lane

When and why did you decide to apply sustainability to your creations?

Sustainability was an integral part of and the fundamental reason behind the founding of Arabel Lebrusan. I started out as a jewellery designer back in 2000, while travelling a lot between Europe and Asia. This is where I really saw the world of jewellery production and the use and abuse of natural materials. At that moment, it was inevitable that I would think about the reasons behind our way of using and abusing Mother Earth to produce and consume. After spending many years designing for other brands and seeing what was going on around me, I decided to start my own jewellery brand. And it was inevitable: my jewellery had to be ethical.

2.26 | The Filigrana collection, made from 100% recycled silver by Arabel Lebrusan

The use of the filigree technique, inspired by the lace work and lightness of the traditional Spanish mantilla, is characteristic of her pieces.

Photo: Akio

Arabel Lebrusan

What difficulties did you experience when you chose to make ethical jewellery?

All of them! The first thing is that no one understood what ethical jewellery is—even other jewellers. Very few people questioned the origins of jewellery or the materials used in it. It is as though by being a luxury item, it can't be problematic.

But the big difficulty was to find suppliers and manufacturers that know where their materials come from: metals and precious stones that are not only conflict free but also have a certificate of origin.

How do you incorporate sustainability into a design?

I simply use materials when I know where they come from and how they have been extracted from the ground. For this reason, I use Fairtrade and Fairmined gold.

However much a particular colour of a precious stone is in fashion, if I don't have a provider for it who can 100% ensure its origin, I don't use it. Being so radical leaves me with few alternatives, but that's an interesting challenge for a designer!

Do you think that the ethical guarantees that you offer are important for your customers?

For my customers, yes; for conventional jewellery customers, not necessarily. That is why it is so important to educate consumers. Once they have all the information, it becomes the only way in which they can buy.

2.27 | Rosette bracelet by Arabel Lebrusan

Piece made from 100% recycled silver and 18k gold plating, using the filigree technique.

Photo: Simon Martner

Do you think that there is potential for sustainable jewellery within the wedding jewellery sector?

I think that there is unlimited potential. An engagement ring represents love between two individuals, a "You are the most beautiful thing that happened in my life," and just the idea that that ring may be tainted by a history of social abuses or by mistreatment of Mother Earth sullies that unique moment.

2.28 | Arabel Lebrusan

Arabel Lebrusan working in her London studio.

Photo: Cat Lane

2.29 | Wedding ring and engagement ring by Arabel Lebrusan

Both pieces are made with Fairtrade-certified 18k white gold.

Photo: Cat Lane

What advice would you give to designers who want to go about their business in a sustainable way?

Begin to ask your suppliers about the origin of all the materials that you use in your jewellery. Produce with workshops that are as close to home as possible. And begin to learn more about the meaning of sustainability and traceability, the two key words when talking about ethical jewellery. When I first started to ask in 2005, there was nothing about responsible jewellery. We were a handful of fanatics who were asking difficult questions, and the answer we got was, "When you work in the jewellery world, you sell your soul to the devil." I refused to accept that that's how it was, and you can too, but we need to do it together to be stronger.

Alliance for Responsible Mining
www.responsiblemines.org

Anna Loucah
www.annaloucah.com

Arabel Lebrusan
www.arabellebrusan.com

Article 22
www.article22.com

Carbon Neutral
www.carbonneutral.com

Diamond Foundry
www.diamondfoundry.com

Global Witness
www.globalwitness.org

Greenpop
www.greenpop.org

Hoover & Strong
www.hooverandstrong.com

Jaume Labro
www.jaumelabro.com

Jersey Pearl
www.jerseypearl.com

María Goti
www.mariagoti.es

Nanini
www.nanini.nl

Nehcaa
nehcaajewelry.com

Rapaport
www.diamonds.net

Ruby Fair
www.rubyfair.com

Soko
www.shopsoko.com

Studio Roosegaarde (Smog Free Project)
www.studioroosegaarde.net

VK Designs
www.valkasinskas.com

3
SUSTAINABLE DESIGN

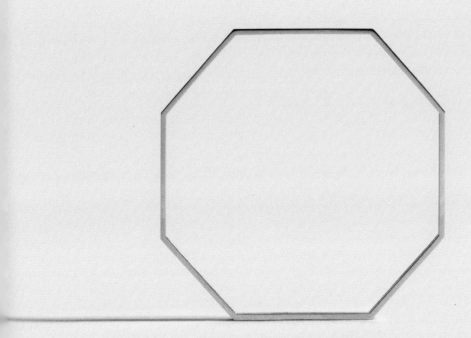

3.1 | Octogone bracelet by JEM
Made from 18k Fairmined gold.
Photo: Victoire Le Tarnec

Motivations

Undertaking a sustainable jewellery project is not an easy task for any designer. This is mainly because, at the moment, it means fighting against the tide. Choosing sustainable solutions entails greater effort and constant searching to be able to continue to offer customers ethical guarantees. Obviously, however, this is not just a matter of customers' perceptions, though we will also see that this aspect is an important one. The most important element always has to be personal motivation, whether it is that of a designer or of a company that is committed to social issues and the environment.

Sincere motivation of this kind is what pushes designers to be concerned about the impact that their activity may have and to take steps to help through jewellery projects.

Taking the path of sustainability when designing a piece of jewellery is a personal act that depends on the mark and the legacy that the designer wishes to leave for the future.

3.2 | Bracelets from the Fluke collection made from 100% recycled silver by Riviera Rebel

British designer Rebecca Oakley had a clear-sighted sustainability philosophy when she set up her Riviera Rebel jewellery firm. The firm's use of recycled metals and sustainable packaging, as well as its donations to the World Wide Fund for Nature from its profits, are part of its ethical commitments.

Photo: Sarah Watkins

A designer's reflections

One important factor to consider before designing a piece of jewellery or a collection is what these activities entail and what resources will be needed to make them possible.

The idea is to analyse each step and evaluate what its impact will be. Depending on the firm or designer, there will be processes that have a greater impact than others, meaning that priorities need to be set when implementing more sustainable alternatives.

It is necessary to analyse each step to evaluate the negative impact that can arise over the supply chain.

Having a start-to-finish overview of the supply chain can also help us to understand how the people involved in each of the required processes interact. With this knowledge, it is possible to arrive at solutions that improve any of these areas, whether they are linked to environmental impact or to social ethics and fair trade.

The firm's philosophy and the designer's awareness must unquestionably be very clear about these issues. Putting into practice the knowledge acquired, investigating existing alternatives and applying creative judgement are ways to come up with formulas that enhance a sustainable form of development that is integrated into the design process from the beginning. This is a better approach than having independent elements that need to be thought about later, as this runs the risk of veering into cosmetic solutions.

Design and artisanship

Sustainable design must also take social well-being into account. By doing so, it is possible to create ties that turn disadvantaged artisans into stakeholders. Industrialization has pushed aside many traditions and craft techniques. This, together with a certain disconnect from the world of contemporary design, makes consumers who are more cosmopolitan or attentive to trends perceive "artisanal" jewellery with some suspicion.

3.3 | La Llanada craftswomen

The most traditional craft techniques from this region of Colombia have been revived by Amalena to offer contemporary jewellery that mixes design qualities with traditions. In this picture are the metalsmiths Natalia Bravo, Elena Montenegro, Adriana Guerrero and Marcela Rodríguez.

Photo: Alexander Rieser

Bringing back craftsmanship by adapting it to changing times and market needs can bring added value to jewellery at the same time as engaging in fair trade activities that help the development and well-being of the groups involved. Artisanal products made by hand but with a design-based approach are undoubtedly becoming more valued.

Many designers who formerly used industrial processes to produce their creations have chosen to use artisanal techniques. Quality and exclusivity are attractive to consumers who are looking for a product that is different and not mass produced.

The jewellery firm Amalena produces its pieces in collaboration with craftswomen from La Llanada in Colombia. Their traditional filigree technique has been adapted by the firm to offer a contemporary product that is also faithful to its local roots. One of Amalena's goals is to offer business opportunities to groups located in isolated regions so that they can generate an income and improve their living conditions.

This objective of fair trade seeks to bring visibility and empowerment to craftswomen so that their art is appreciated and so that they feel proud of it. At the same time, the firm incorporates a technique that is conditioned by these craftswomen into its design process.

Emotional ties

Establishing emotional ties with consumers is a fundamental aspect throughout the design process, so a briefing must always contain information about our target customers and take into account their habits, tastes and needs. In a design process that takes into account sustainability from the very beginning, we have to study how the jewellery piece will interact with the wearer, and how consumers will find added value to invest their emotions in.

To make this possible, we have to design a product that is capable of attracting attention and becoming an object of desire, not only because of its beauty but also because of the meaning and values that the traceability of the materials used represents, the contribution of the people involved in each process, the artisanal or innovative value of the manufacturing techniques, or the contribution made to solving social issues.

We are still very far from the point where every good act can excite and appeal to society on a mass scale, but it is undeniable that there is a potential audience willing to feel empathy over a jewellery piece whose value goes beyond merely being an adornment.

3.4 | Two artisans who work with the firm Article 22 in Laos

Offering emotional values creates ties with consumers and causes them to opt for a jewellery piece that respects the environment. It is also important for them to know the stories that are behind each piece or the material used. The beauty of the design is essential in allowing all these values to have a positive impact and turns it into an object of desire.

Photo: Article 22

Connecting with the consumer

Designer Ana Khouri connects with audiences both through the elegance of her pieces and through communicating a very clear message that is part of the jewellery's essence. The pieces only contain raw materials with a clear traceability in order to provide an ethical product. The success of the brand shows that high jewellery does not have to be incompatible with sustainability. Traceable metals, conflict-free gems and local craftsmanship make this firm an example of how the values deposited in a gem are enhanced by a sustainable design.

3.5

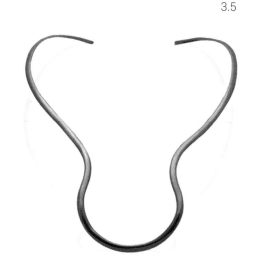

3.5 | Simplicity necklace by Ana Khouri

Made from 18k certified Fairtrade gold, which guarantees that the origin of the metal is linked to fair trade practices and environmental conservation.

Photo: Brain Dolphin

3.6 | Simplicity rigid bracelet by Ana Khouri

Bracelet made from 18k certified Fairtrade gold with ethically sourced natural white diamonds.

Photo: Christophe Berlet

3.6

3.7 - 3.8 | Pendant and bracelet by the French firm JEM Jewellery Ethically Minded

All of JEM's jewellery is made from 18 k Fairmined-certified gold and incorporates a serial number that provides traceability for the whole supply chain.

Photo: Victoire Le Tarnec

Another way of making an emotional connection with consumers is to ensure that each piece is unique and different, thereby making them part of a transparent and ethical supply chain. Based on this idea, JEM Jewellery Ethically Minded has incorporated into each of its pieces a unique serial number that allows consumers to trace the materials—in this case, Fairmined-certified sustainable gold—back to their origins. The firm's policy on the use of ethical raw materials is very clear, and this determines its designs, since at the moment they refrain from using diamonds on the basis that they have not yet received sufficient guarantees about their traceability. However, JEM continues to study new possibilities with suppliers of diamonds and coloured stones that meet its standards.

Designing and providing solutions

A value proposition will unquestionably provide concrete solutions that offer new opportunities to marginalized groups. Jewellery has become focused on human factors in this respect. Reflecting on issues that require a solution can open new paths when designing a jewellery piece or when getting a firm off the ground.

Based on this premise, Caterina Occhio created the project SeeMe, a jewellery-firm concept based above all on ethical values.

Although it is not linked to the use of sustainable raw materials, its strategy is focused on undertaking fair trade activities on the social and labour levels, where jewellery is but an instrument.

Its efforts are focused on offering a profession and employment to women who have been victims of violence and who are socially excluded in their communities. They are normally single mothers from Tunisia and Lebanon who do not have a professional background and who are completely discriminated against because of who they are, since single motherhood in these countries leads to general rejection.

3.9 | Caterina Occhio
Founder of SeeMe.
Photo: © 2016 SeeMe, Ethical Jewelry

3.10 | Silver pendant by SeeMe
Pendant with a large silver heart.
Photo: © 2016 SeeMe, Ethical Jewelry

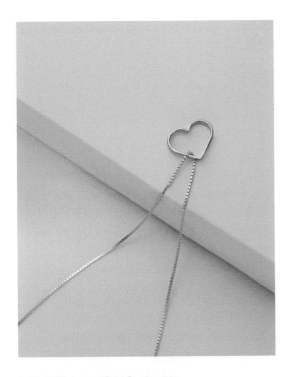

These women are trained in the profession from scratch, since they do not have any previous experience in jewellery production. This detail also conditions the design, since the jewellery pieces are not overly complex. Their design takes a simple form that is connected to the brand's principles, with the heart being the element of inspiration in all its collections.

SeeMe's great efforts have caught the attention of the big names in fashion, resulting in collaborations with brands such as Karl Lagerfeld, Missoni and Tommy Hilfiger.

3.11 | Silver pendant by SeeMe
Small heart pendant made from .925 silver with gold plating and Venetian chain.
Photo: © 2016 SeeMe, Ethical Jewelry

3.12 | Tunisian craftswoman working with SeeMe
Thanks to SeeMe's collaboration with the association AMAL POUR LA FAMILLE ET L'ENFANT and the company BIJOUX MODERNE TUNIS, many women have been able to find a job and learn a profession, a factor that gives them dignity and helps them to overcome their exclusion. This is an example of empowering women through fair trade practices.
Photo: © 2016 SeeMe, Ethical Jewelry

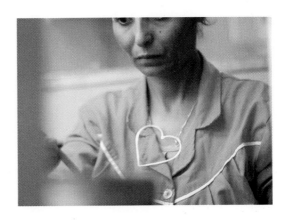

The Supply Chain

To appreciate the potential impact that the activities involved in creating a piece of jewellery can have, it is very important to understand the setup of the supply chain, which includes all the processes required to design, manufacture and sell a collection. As we will see later, there are many factors involved, directly and indirectly, to make this possible. We will begin by analysing the raw materials that will be used.

Having an accurate knowledge of a material's origins and how it has been processed so that it can be comfortably used in a jewellery workshop is a decisive factor in establishing a strategy that can reduce negative impacts. And having an in-depth knowledge of the possible problems that lie behind each material will lead to a search for and investigation of existing alternatives.

The following chapters delve into the most commonly used raw materials in jewellery and each one's impact at an environmental and social level. We will also see what alternatives and solutions are available.

Recycling as a sustainable basis

Recycling is a practice that has been used since jewellery has existed, as metals such as gold or silver can be recycled as many times as desired without there being an effect on their properties. Once cast into ingots, it is not possible to tell if the metal was recycled or freshly mined, since its chemical composition is exactly the same.

Understanding the impact of raw materials can affect the decisions to be made when designing a jewellery piece so that more sustainable alternatives are sought out.

3.13 | Ring by Jaume Labro made from recycled metals

Ring made from 100% recycled and certified 18k white and yellow gold from the Japanese company Sato Kin Gin.

Photo: Jaume Labro

Creative recycling

But recycling can also be used as a basis for design by using materials or objects that had nothing to do with jewellery in their previous life but that can nevertheless be reused creatively, transforming them and elevating them to the category of jewellery.

This is known as "upcycling." Unlike in recycling, the materials are not transformed or broken down to be used again. Instead, the same raw material is used, but its original function is changed.

3.14 | Pendant by Maral Raap

The North American firm Maral Raap reuses brass mesh by the iconic firm Whiting & Davis to make its jewellery. All its pieces are handmade and plated in 14K gold.

Photo: Maral Rapp

3.15 | Maral Raap earrings by Camilla Pietropaoli

As a foundation for creating her jewellery, the Italian designer Camilla Pietropaoli uses broken bicycle inner tubes. In a completely different context, rubber combined with pieces of silver takes on another meaning.

Photo: Camilla Pietropaoli

The most widely used materials in these cases are derived from petroleum, which does not biodegrade easily. When there are very small parts, they may end up scattered everywhere.

Giving new life to products that are no longer in use is definitely a sustainable practice because new raw materials are not required in the production process, which contributes to eliminating waste that would most likely end up in a landfill or in places where it can have a polluting effect on the ecosystem.

3.16 - 3.17 | My Milk necklace and bracelet by Cherry Boonyapan
To make this necklace and bracelet, the designer used the seals from the lids of Tetra Pak milk cartons, which have no further use once the carton is open. The collection is part of the Spreeglanz project (Berlin), a platform for new talents.

Photo: Peter Lorenz

New life for rubbish

Another project that also fulfils the characteristics of upcycling is that by the electrical goods firm Balay and the jewellery designer Elena Estaun. This initiative is a surprising one, since the original idea came from a group of assembly-line employees after they saw that there was always a surplus of small pieces that are normally used in the manufacture of various appliances and that end up in the company's recycling process.

Thanks to their creativity and inventiveness, along with Elena Estaun's experience as a designer, it was possible to create a jewellery collection that aimed to raise funds through sales for those in greatest need, with the team collaborating with the Adunare Foundation on assistance projects such as soup kitchens.

3.18 | Creative team for the Balay jewellery collection project

Designer Elena Estaun along with the team behind the idea: Ana Isabel Salillas, Victoria Alegre, Celia Añón, Irene Sancerni and Nuria González.

Photo: BSH Electrodomésticos España, S.A.

3.19 | Pendant by Balay

The necklace is made of a metallic piece with rubber that was recycled at Balay's electrical-goods plants. Both the piece and the brass chain are gold plated.

Photo: BSH Electrodomésticos España, S.A.

3.19

Article 22

Article 22 is a jewellery firm located in New York City. It was founded in 2012 by Elizabeth Suda and Camile Hautefort. The outcome of the spirit of solidarity that its brand values and philosophy are based on was its first jewellery collection, called Peacebomb. This initiative is a clear example of projects that are created out of the need to offer social engagement as a main objective. It involved significant work on justice and human rights and it coexists in perfect balance with the most avant-garde fashion, an aspect that contemporary consumers find difficult to give up.

To understand the brand's essence, it is necessary to go back in time to the terrible events that took place in Laos, the most heavily bombed country in the world. During the so-called "Secret War," a collateral conflict to the Vietnam War that took place between 1964 and 1973, the US Army dropped between 250 and 260 million bombs, which is the equivalent of a B-52 bombing attack every 8 minutes, 24 hours a day, for 9 years.

3.20 | Camile Hautefort and Elizabeth Suda, founders of Article 22

Photo: Article 22

3.21 | Bracelets by Article 22

Bracelets from the Buying Back the Bombs campaign next to antipersonnel mines, the aluminium of which is extracted to make the bracelets.

Photo: Article 22

This cruel and unjust war is not just a reminder of the past, since antipersonnel mines are still having a big impact on the lives and development of the local population. It is surprising to visit some of the country's villages, and in particular the closest ones to the border with Vietnam. In these places, the residents have incorporated leftover ordnance into their everyday lives. They decorate the entrances to buildings and are part of improvised furniture such as seats, tables and flowerpot stands.

Many of the local craftspeople have found countless uses for all of these remains from the war that have been part of the landscape for several decades, including the manufacturing of spoons with the metal recycled from bombs that have been located and defused.

3.22 | Craftsperson in Laos

A craftsperson using moulds into which molten aluminium is poured to create spoons.

Photo: Article 22

3.23 | Aluminium bracelet by Article 22

The aluminium body of this bracelet comes from recycling the landmines that remain hidden in the fields and rice paddies of Laos.

Photo: Article 22

Article 22

3.24

3.25

The founders of Article 22 learned about this fascinating history, and through Elizabeth's social engagement and Camile's entrepreneurial streak, they developed a brand based on respectful manufacturing, recycling, artisanship and the value of human rights. Using the same manufacturing process as that used to make spoons, Article 22 designed bracelets made entirely by local craftspeople through ancestral jewellery techniques and recycled metal from bombs as the primary material.

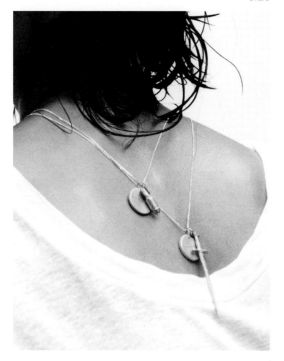

3.26

3.24 - 3.25 | Bracelets made by Article 22 from recycled aluminium

Article 22 allocates a percentage of the profits from the sale of this jewellery to collaborations with different NGOs to clear antipersonnel mines in the areas of Laos most affected by them.

Photo: Article 22

3.26 | Love or Perish pendant by Article 22

This pendant suggests a story of the transformation of a bomb into an object that offers new opportunities to an unfairly punished people.

Photo: Article 22

3.27 | Elizabeth Suda

Elizabeth Suda working with a craftsperson in Laos.

Photo: Article 22

In addition to providing decent work for these artisans, the firm also works directly with various NGOs, including MAG, which carries out its charitable activities in these villages. Article 22's commitment takes the form of allocating for each bracelet or jewellery piece sold sufficient resources to clear mines for a 3 m² area. Many bombs have not been defused and remain hidden, and they continue to inflict death and mutilation on the region's inhabitants.

3.27

Amalena
www.amalena.com

Ana Khouri
www.anakhouri.com

Article 22
article22.com

Balay
www.balay.es

Camilla Pietropaoli
www. camillapi.com

Cherry Boonyapan
www.cherryboonyapan.com

Elena Estaun
www.elenaestaun.com

Jaume Labro
www.jaumelabro.com

JEM Jewellery Ethical Minded
www.jem-paris.com

Karl Lagerfeld
www.karl.com

MAG
www.maginternational.org

Maral Rapp
www.maralrapp.com

Missoni
www.missoni.com

Riviera Rebel
rivierarebel.co.uk

SeeMe
www.seeme.org

Tommy Hilfiger
global.tommy.com

4
RAW
MATERIALS

4.1 | Rings by Soko

Rings made by artisans in Kenya from recycled metals.

Photo: Jana Cruder

Most raw materials used in making jewellery are closely linked to mining, an activity based on the extraction of nonrenewable materials.

These mining activities involve various stages, each of which has a significant environmental, social and cultural impact. These stages are prospecting, preparing the land, exploiting and, finally, processing the minerals so that they can be used.

The damaging effects produced by each of these different stages are deforestation, destruction of ecosystems and the disproportionate consumption of natural resources. Then there are the health risks and the working conditions that many people in the industry are subjected to.

Each of the stages has a negative impact that in some respects will always be part of jewellery making. For this reason, it is necessary to understand the impact of each of the raw materials that we use and know about the materials' origin and the different processes undertaken before the piece reaches us. This information gives us the power to make certain decisions and think about alternatives when it comes to designing and creating a jewellery piece.

4.2 | A gold mining operation
Locals in Cajamarca, Peru, assessing the impact of gold mining on their land.
Photo: Malú Cabellos

Metals

Large-scale mining

The quintessential and most frequently used noble metals in the jewellery world are gold and silver. The industrialized extraction of these involves mines that are created through excavating or exploding rock, which always takes place following a geological study carried out to ascertain if the rocks contain the metals. This has a big impact on the areas and regions where mining operations are set up, since huge quantities of the earth are removed and polluted. River courses are altered and farming activities are curtailed. The development of indigenous communities is also affected, and they are forced to abandon the place where they were born and raised, something which leads little by little to the disappearance of many aboriginal cultures and populations.

Understanding the impact and origin of raw materials gives us the power to make certain decisions and think about alternatives when it comes to designing and creating a jewellery piece.

But the extraction of metals always brings with it a high risk of pollution of land and water through toxic elements, since the use of acids and cyanide is a standard practice for separating gold or silver from other minerals. Alternatively, different chemical reagents such as lime and flocculants are deployed in the case of copper, a metal used to make alloys such as brass.

As for platinum, chemical reagents, which normally take the form of powerful acids, are also used to separate the platinum particles from the other materials and different metals.

4.3 | Gold refining

Fort Knox installations belonging to the Kinross corporation in Alaska, USA.

Photo: Kinross Gold Corporation

73

Extraction and processing produce a large volume of waste that is contaminated by the toxic elements, and this waste is stored in dumps, which creates the risk of leakage into the ground that can contaminate underground water reserves.

The extent of this impact is difficult to calculate on a general level with certainty. Depending on the country, its laws, its environmental policies and even the regulations followed by each business, the result may be different, and this may further add to our confusion.

Aside from pollution from toxic substances, there is also environmental pollution from the large-scale consumption of water and high CO_2 emissions.

4.4

4.5

4.4 | Transportation of minerals

The trucks transport the mineral extracted from the mine for processing.
Akara Resources, Phichit-Phetchabun, Tailandia.

Photo: Krittathat Taveetanathada

4.5 | The environmental impact of gold extraction

Obtaining a gram of gold produces 20 kg of CO_2 and 2,500 kg of waste, and it consumes 2,500 litres of water.

4.6 | Poster for the documentary Daughter of the Lake

Documentary produced by Guarango Film & Video. Directed by Ernesto Cabellos Damián.

Poster designed by Javier Piragauta.

Daughter of the Lake

Ernesto Cabellos's documentary Hija de la laguna (Daughter of the Lake) offers a clear example of how large-scale gold mining is taking hold in countries such as Peru, where local communities are forced to give up their natural resources and made to leave their homes and land because of the heavy pressure that large business groups and corporations exert on governments. The documentary offers a broad and up-to-date view of the problems related to the mining corporations that operate in the Andes mountain range in Peru. The documentary's central figure, Nelida Ayay, gives us a first-person account of the vulnerability of rural communities in the face of the gold rush.

Jewellery designer Bibi van der Velden also took part in the documentary

www.daughterofthelake.pe

Prizes and distinctions

· Mark Haslam Prize - Planet in Focus Environmental Film Festival, Toronto, Canada.
· Audience Award - Latinamerika i Fokus Film Festival, Malmö, Sweden.
· Best Documentary - Festival de Cine Documental Atlantidoc, Atlántida, Uruguay.
· Tunki Prize for Best Peruvian Documentary of 2015, Lima, Peru.
· DOCLA Special Mention for Courage and Activism for protagonist Nelida Ayay, Los Angeles, USA.
· Special Jury Mention, Présence Autochtone, Montreal, 2016.
· SIGNIS Prize, Festival de Cine Ambiental FINCA, Buenos Aires, 2016.
· Best Documentary Prize, Festival de la Memoria, Morelos, 2016.

Small-scale mining

Because illegal mining is not regulated by any organization, it has devastating consequences on the environment through polluting earth, air and water with highly toxic elements that also harm public health.

As we have already seen, in artisanal and small-scale mining, the process of separating gold from other minerals such as sand and mud uses mercury. This process produces an amalgam in which gold dust and particles mix with the mercury. It is then filtered and melted, and the mercury evaporates, releasing the gold contained within.

The mercury vapour comes back to the ground through rain, contaminating practically everything. The metals that these illegal mining operations extract are sold on the black market, and they are then absorbed into the global market, so neither their origins nor their extraction method can ever be identified.

4.7 | Mercury use

A miner handling mercury to create an amalgam with the extracted gold.

Photo: Mauricio Vélez

4.8 | Mercury evaporation

In this process, the amalgam is heated until the mercury evaporates, revealing the gold.

Photo: Mauricio Vélez

But the damaging impact of this type of illegal mining goes beyond what is caused by this environmental pollution, since the landscape is also devastated. The use of backhoes to deforest huge areas destroys the biodiversity of ecosystems in a way that is very difficult to repair.

Another significant impact is that produced on the social level, since in the vicinity of each mining operation immense settlements are created where alcohol and prostitution are widespread, which creates marginalization that also affects the children who live there.

4.9 | Aerial image of deforestation caused by illegal mining
The illegal mining of gold in Colombia has created a major environmental pollution problem along the Río Quito area of Chocó. Bit by bit, one of the world's most precious tropical forests is being destroyed.
Photo: Mauricio Vélez

Gems

Gems are another kind of raw material used in jewellery making.

The gem industry is also linked to mining, and it is the subject of great controversy, as we have seen earlier, because of its connections with all manner of human rights violations such as forced labour, slavery and child exploitation.

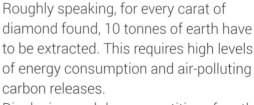

Roughly speaking, for every carat of diamond found, 10 tonnes of earth have to be extracted. This requires high levels of energy consumption and air-polluting carbon releases.
Displacing such large quantities of earth also causes water and soil pollution owing to leakage of toxic substances. All this creates an imbalance that affects the area's ecosystem and puts the survival of indigenous ecosystems at risk.

Depending on the mining company's agreements with the country in which exploitation is being conducted, measures are taken to reduce this impact through energy-efficiency and pollution-control programmes, replacement of top soils to conserve the ecosystem, and seeding of the area once the mining has come to an end.

Diamonds

Industrial mining for diamonds also has a big environmental impact at the sites where it takes place, as open-pit mining requires deforestation of large areas, the use of explosives on rocks and large-scale movements of earth.

4.10 | Diamond
Brilliant-cut diamond.
Photo: Jedidja / pixabay.com

Coloured stones

In contrast to the extraction of diamonds and precious metals, 80% of coloured gems come from artisanal or small-scale mining, which means that this industry is subject to very little control. The working conditions of the people involved are highly precarious and dangerous, and there are multiple injuries and deaths each year due to the sector's practices, which in many cases may be illegal. By contrast, an analysis of the supply chain reveals that distributors, manufacturers and traders always make the greatest profits, as opposed to the people who risk their lives to extract the gems from the earth.

In terms of the processing of coloured gems, another significant aspect is the alteration of stones to improve their qualities. This practice has become so widespread that it is an everyday part of the industry, without consideration being given to the harmful impact on the environment.

With the aim of increasing their beauty or economic value, coloured gems are exposed to different processes that intensify their transparency, clarity or colour and reduce imperfections or impurities that the stone might contain.

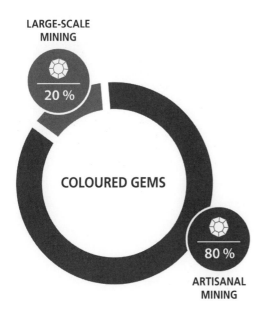

LARGE-SCALE
MINING

20 %

COLOURED GEMS

80 %

ARTISANAL
MINING

4.11 | Mining of coloured gems

In total, 80% of the world's extraction of coloured stones takes place through artisanal mining.

These changes are carried out by subjecting the stones to temperature changes or radiation, or through the application of chemical substances.

This creates a delicate situation, as aside from the natural resources required, the practices used to improve the quality of coloured stones are linked to the use of nuclear reactors or chemical elements and dyes that, if not properly controlled, can cause serious pollution problems.

Coloured gems are exposed to radiation or chemical substances in order to improve their appearance.

One of the gems to most frequently be treated with irradiation to change its colour is topaz, whose intense blue colour is unusual in nature. For this reason, most topaz available on the market has been subjected to radiation and subsequent heating, with the goal of producing a wide range of highly intense blue tones.

Other coloured gems that irradiation processes of this kind are usually applied to include quartz, beryl, spodumene and fluorite.

It should be pointed out that many diamonds are often subjected to this process to acquire so-called "fancy" tones and different colours.

Gems that are generally usually dyed to give them a greater intensity or a wide colour range are agate, lapis lazuli, chalcedony, jade, ruby, emerald, quartz and sapphire.

4.12 | Coloured gem
Oval-cut ruby.
Photo: Mathieu Kessler / pixabay.com

High-risk and illegal raw materials

Some primary materials have been used in jewellery for a long time, but as the years have gone by and with unrestrained and abusive use of them, they have become high-risk raw materials because of their harmful impact.

The extensive use of coral to make jewellery has caused destruction that has destabilized the marine ecosystem and created environmental problems. For this reason, it is completely illegal to extract or trade in it in many countries.

Ivory and turtle shell are raw materials that are considered to be illegal in almost every country, but poaching still takes place and continues to have a destructive impact. Taking elephants' tusks for sale on the black market causes the indiscriminate death of more than 50,000 elephants each year in Africa.

Some designers are using ivory from mammoth remains as an ethical alternative, as this animal has been extinct for almost 4,000 years.

4.13 | Coral reef

Due to the laws that protect coral reefs, it is very difficult to find suppliers that operate on a completely legal basis. As a result, it has become a high-risk material that lacks a transparent supply chain. For this reason, in 2002 Tiffany decided to stop using coral in its collections.

Photo: joakant / pixabay.com

Lower-impact materials

Using any raw material will always have a certain impact. The idea is to make that impact as small as possible.

When we talk about sustainable or more sustainable raw materials, we are referring to the much smaller size of their footprint, at the levels of both society and ecosystems, since in their extraction and development not only is there consideration of the greatest economic return possible, but respect for the environment and the communities involved is also seen as essential and logical. The aim is to create a clear and transparent supply chain, in order to produce fairer and more equitative benefits in terms of natural resources, the people and the environment.

Through different initiatives, projects and organizations, various certifications for the most widely used raw materials in jewellery such as different metals and gems have been created. Each certification entails specific guarantees that ensure traceability from the mine to each designer's or jeweller's work space.

Sustainable raw materials

- Minimize environmental impact
- Reduce the consumption of resources
- Create social responsibility
- Are distributed through fair trade

4.14 | Necklace from the Aire collection by Majoral

Spanish firm Majoral backs the use of sustainable materials under the Fairmined Gold and Fairmined Silver certifications. Majoral is also a distributor with a Fairmined licence for Spain.

Photo: Martin Azúa

Sustainable and ecological metals

As we have seen, various ethical problems hide behind precious metals. For this reason, the different certifications for sustainable metals, which arose through the pioneering Green Gold project, aim to offer traceability and guarantees for each gram of gold, silver or platinum from its leaving the mine to its reaching the end consumer. These guarantees and traceability are based on standards that promote organizational development, social development, environmental protection and decent working conditions.

Fairmined
Yves Bertran · Executive Director
Alliance for Responsible Mining

Fairmined is a standard and assurance mark that certifies gold from responsible artisanal and small-scale mining organizations. Through this standard, any jewellery brand that buys Fairmined gold can work with a traceable product that comes from responsible sources. This contributes to the development of artisanal mines and the families and communities connected to them, and it has a positive impact on responsible mining.

The Fairmined standard supports the sustainable development of mining organizations, providing stimuli for them to become viable businesses that carry out their activities in an economically, technologically and environmentally responsible way. Moreover, it facilitates access to fair markets, provides a prize for development and benefits mining communities.

Fairmined is backed by a rigorous third-party certification system and by an audit system that ensures that small mining organizations implement internationally recognized responsible practices.

At the end of 2016, more than 130 jewellers in 21 countries worked with Fairmined Gold, *the gold to be proud of*.

The Fairmined initiative was created by the Alliance for Responsible Mining, a Colombian NGO that is recognized worldwide as a pioneer for its work with responsible artisanal and small-scale mining.

Recycled metals

It should be stressed that, when it comes to recycling, the jewellery sector has been a pioneer of this practice for thousands of years. But we should not deceive ourselves, since it could be said that this recycling has always been a matter of convenience that results from high metal prices. Every gram of gold or silver is carefully collected and stored in order to be melted down once again. The fact that these metals are easy to melt down has contributed to the traditional recycling of them by everyone from artisans to large refining plants.

The objective of using recycled metals is to reduce the impact that the mining industry has, whether at a small scale or a large one. Our use of recycled metals indirectly contributes to reducing the use of the chemicals required in the extraction of new metals from mines.

If when we purchase gold or silver to make jewellery it lacks certification that gives a transparent guarantee regarding the supply chain, it is very difficult to know about its origins. As a result, it is important to be able to turn to suppliers that work with certifiably 100% recycled metals.

The recycling of precious metals for jewellery is a very old practice, but we must not forget that it was done for reasons of convenience.

4.15 | Earrings by Toby Pomeroy

North American designer Toby Pomeroy was a pioneer in demanding that his metal supplier, Hoover & Strong, provide him with 100% recycled gold and silver. He did this at a time when it was not the norm. This cooperation between the two firms began in 2006 and raised awareness in a way that has made certified 100% recycled metals one of the most attractive things that Hoover & Strong has to offer its customers.

Photo: Michael Cuiccio

Normally, at refineries and some suppliers, recycled metal ends up being mixed with freshly mined metal, which means that any jewellery firm that uses conventional metals may say that it is using recycled metals. However, this would be false advertising, as in fact there can be no certainty about what proportion is recycled relative to what is not, and nor can there be any about the way in which the relevant processes were carried out. And, worse still, this approach does not provide any solution that has a less harmful impact.

When it comes to recycled metals, we have to accept guarantees that allow us to know about the metal's exact origins and processing methods, and these must be subject to different forms of audit. When we reach a point where metals are 100% recycled and fulfil all the environmental and labour requirements and have traceability that can be certified, we will truly be able to say that those metals are more sustainable and that their use in jewellery making reduces the mining industry's environmental and social impact.

Where to buy 100% recycled metals

Metal suppliers and businesses that have their own marks and certifications for metals such as 100% recycled gold, silver and platinum include Hoover & Strong, Stuller, United Precious Metals, A&E Metals, Umicore and Vipa Design. Cookson Gold and its Spanish subsidiary Sempsa have the EcoSilver mark and different certifications, which provide a guarantee that their metals are 100% recycled. The metals are available in formats that include plates, threads, tubes and grains.

4.16 | EcoSilver

A plate of 100% recycled EcoSilver silver by Cookson Gold.

Photo: Cookson Precious Metals Ltd.

Fairmined Gold
Fairmined Platinum
Fairmined Silver

The Fairmined initiative was created by the Alliance for Responsible Mining, which is recognized across the world as a pioneer in responsible artisanal and small-scale mining. It represents a significant development opportunity for artisanal and small-scale miners all over the world. Promoting these miners as formal operations and easing their access to fair markets helps them to improve their practices and to bring about improvements in their communities.

Fairmined certifications for gold, platinum and silver offer clear traceability for metal that comes from artisanal and small-scale mining operations that work on a legal and organized basis and respect the environment through the controlled use of chemical substances, with the aim of gradually reducing the use of these.

Fairmined Eco Gold
Fairmined Eco Platinum
Fairmined Eco Silver

The Fairmined Eco certifications for gold, platinum and silver offer clear traceability for metal that comes from artisanal and small-scale mining operations that work on a legal and organized basis and respect the environment through using no chemical substances at all, and through using only gravimetric methods to separate the metal from other minerals.

They also include reforestation programmes that restore native ecosystems.

Fairtrade Gold
Fairtrade Platinum
Fairtrade Silver

100% recycled metals

The mines that produce Fairtrade gold and precious metals are located in South America and Africa. The first certification was awarded in October 2016 to a mine in Uganda. One of the most important conditions of the Fairtrade standards is the requirement to operate without child labour so that children can attend school and avoid exposure to health and safety risks. It can take mines several years to receive Fairtrade certification, and during that period, the miners receive a fair wage from the moment when the process begins. Through this process, the miners can look after their families and enjoy reasonable working hours rather than long shifts. Safety training and health checks are carried out frequently. Fairtrade requirements such as safe handling and reduction of harmful substances that are used in mining—for example, mercury and cyanide—take time to implement but bring the miners safety and protect water supplies, including stream channels.

SCS Global Services promotes care for the environment and social responsibility. It awards certifications to different businesses, and it conducts audits to provide reliable proof that their metals are 100% recycled, that they protect the environment and that they deploy ethical working practices.

Cookson's EcoSilver is accredited by ISO 9001, ISO 14001 and OHSAS 18001. These guarantee a metal's status as 100% recycled and safeguard environmental impact, safety and best labour practices.

So that the different gems used in jewellery fit sustainability standards, the main objective is to be able to rely on a defined and transparent form of traceability, first of all so that gems do not come from conflict zones where slavery and human rights violations may take place. This means that each gem must come with certification that guarantees its origins and not just its quality.

As we know, there are many controversies surrounding precious stones, since even with initiatives such as the Kimberley Process, it has not been possible to guarantee the legitimate origins of many diamonds that are still sold nowadays.

Conflict-free diamonds

Any jewellery firm that wishes to use transparent practices must give its backing to conflict-free diamonds. Because the traceability of these gems continues to be a problem in many African countries, the use of diamonds from Canada and Australia has increased.

But as is the case in any sector, different types of deception can take place. For example, not all Canadian diamonds come from Canada. These gems undergo long journeys to be cut and polished in places such as India or China, which can give rise to bogus audits. As a result, it is important to be able to turn to independent audits and certifications such as CanadaMark™, which guarantees diamonds' origins and ensures that the cutting and polishing are also carried out in the country of origin.

These certifications additionally guarantee that responsibility has also been taken to reduce negative environmental impact.

4.17 | Ring by Fair Trade Jewellery Co
Engagement ring made from 18k platinum and a 1.01ct Sirius Star® Canadian diamond with CanadaMark™ certification.
Photo: Kathleen Kerr/FTJCo.

In Australia or Canada, natural diamonds that can be acquired through suppliers such as Origin Australia® or Inspira Diamonds come from the Argyle mine, which is operated by large mining companies that aim for sustainable practices to protect the ecosystem and the local communities.

Having a guarantee that diamonds come from countries such as Canada, Australia or Russia ensures that they are not blood diamonds, which are a problem that has had disastrous effects.

Moreover, mining firms located in these places work with their respective governments to offer solutions, in the form of environmental and social programmes, to the impact that mining has.

Another way of guaranteeing that diamonds and gems conform to a high ethical standard comes from the organization Rapaport Fair Trade. This is an initiative that aims to create fair and efficient markets that increase transparency within the diamond industry.

To this end, Rapaport Ethical Certification was created. This monitoring system is verified by third parties, and it traces diamonds from the mine to the jeweller. Through doing so, it can review whether there have been any human rights abuses or other ethical issues over the course of the supply chain.

4.18 | Rough pink diamond
The Argyle Pink Jubilee Diamond is the biggest rough pink diamond to be discovered in Australia.
Photo: © 2016 Rio Tinto

Naturally coloured stones

One characteristic of coloured gems is the labelling of their origin. It is well known that the majority of emeralds come from Colombia, and that most rubies and sapphires respectively come from Myanmar and Sri Lanka. However, this information does not guarantee the conditions under which they have been extracted. As has previously been suggested here, 80% of the mining of coloured stones is controlled by artisanal and small-scale operations, which in most cases operate illegally in all their aspects.

The few large-scale mining firms involved in this system offer greater control over the supply chain and more transparent traceability to the market than artisanal mining operations do. One example is the firm Gemfields, which carries out industrialized operations in countries such as Zambia, offering better infrastructure and decent working conditions as it does so.

Sadly, the honesty and reputation of coloured gems suppliers continues to be one of the few endorsements of ethical practices.

4.19 | Ring by Melville
Fairtrade 18k white gold with blue sapphires and natural diamonds.
Photo: © Melville Fine Jewellery

But the big problem with coloured gems is that they are not backed by any official certification similar to Fairmined or Fairtrade in the case of metals, or to the diamond market's Kimberley Process. This state of affairs produces an ethical and legal void in which the only guarantee stems from the trust in and the word of each supplier, with reputation and honesty continuing to be among the few forms of endorsement.

One of the most important sustainability characteristics is the stone's not being submitted to any improvement process involving heat, dye or radiation. As we have already seen, these processes unnecessarily consume energy and resources that also pollute the environment. Any competent gemmological laboratory can determine if a given stone has been treated with one of these methods, which makes it possible to know if we have been conned during our purchase. But the best way to avoid deception and to be sure is to deal with providers that will guarantee from the outset the natural state of the gems offered and that will always provide certificates from independent laboratories with the stones.

One such provider is Ruby Fair, which in addition to providing completely natural rubies, sapphires, spinels and tanzanites also ensures that the origin of the stones is completely ethical in terms of social and ecological practices. Columbia Gem House and Nineteen48 also offer natural gems with ethical origins, though some of the gems that can be found in their catalogues have been heat treated, and this is always specified where it is the case.

4.20 | Earrings by The Rock Hound made from recycled 18k white gold and coated in nanoceramics. The gems used include demantoid, morganite and kunzite of ethical origins

The Rock Hound applies very strict ethical standards to source its metals and gems in a responsible way. Its suppliers' code of conduct allows it to maintain these values through a transparent supply chain. The gems that the firm uses are from Brazil, Tanzania, Sri Lanka, Australia and Canada.

Photo: AC Cooper

4.21 | Diamond Foundry

Diamond Foundry is a business from California that has pioneered the laboratory creation of diamonds. Stones of this kind do not invite doubts about their origin (as there is no chance of involvement by intermediaries with questionable reputations), and they have a very low carbon footprint because of the use of renewable energy in the process.

Photo: Diamond Foundry Inc.

Laboratory-produced diamonds

Diamonds and gems created in a laboratory do not have the same hardness and quality as natural diamonds. The difference between the two types results from the fact that the latter type requires a natural process that has occurred over thousands of years. Opponents of artificial diamonds argue that they can destabilize the market owing to their lower price. By contrast, pioneering businesses in this sector such as Diamond Foundry or Pure Grown Diamonds assert that there is great market potential for manmade diamonds, since the conventional diamond industry has lost many customers over the past decade because of its questionable ethics.

But regardless of such controversy, what is true is that diamonds that are not the product of mining also do not come from conflict zones, finance wars or destroy the environment through the effects of mining. This has brought about a shift in the general perception of diamonds from the point of view of ethics and sustainability. Given the circumstances, no sustainable jewellery firm in the sector would hide the fact that the diamonds that it sells have been produced in a laboratory or attempt to deceive the consumer by passing them off as natural diamonds. In fact, this type of diamond has become attractive to new generations who do not want to touch gems that may have come from a conflict zone.

4.22 | Plasma reactor

Photo: Diamond Foundry Inc.

4.23 | Laboratory-made diamonds

Photo: Diamond Foundry Inc.

Lower-impact pearls

Scarcity and particular laws that limit oyster fishing for the purposes of obtaining pearls, in combination with the high market demand for them, led more than half a century ago to the practice of growing them, initially in Australia and French Polynesia.

Improvements in these techniques, alongside the proliferation of firms focused on pearl cultivation, have brought about a damaging impact on marine ecosystems, harming coral reefs and marine biodiversity. And the infrastructure required for the procedures also has an impact.

Thanks to organizations such as Sustainable Pearls, projects are being undertaken to make pearl cultivation have a positive impact by encouraging responsible practices to conserve the surrounding environment.

4.24 - 4.25 - 4.26 | Kamoka Pearls is a company that cultivates pearls sustainably

Kamoka Pearls carefully respects the fragility of the ecosystem by using clean energy and cultivation practices that do not harm marine biodiversity or the life of the oysters. Its pearls are also not subjected to any kind of treatment to alter their colour, and the nucleus used to produce the pearl within the oyster is made from mother of pearl.

Ethical labour conditions are also part of its philosophy, and the company supports social development in Tahiti, where the business operates.

Photos: Josh Humbert

4.27 | Octopus brooch by Tiffany made from platinum with pavé diamonds and pearls from Tahiti

In 2000, this prestigious firm created the foundation Tiffany & Co. Among many of its activities to support sustainable development, it collaborates with SustainablePearls.org in the sustainable cultivation of pearls in Tahiti.

Photo: Carlton Davis

Secondary materials

Jewellery making also involves the use of materials other than metals and gems. Although we might describe these as "secondary," we must evaluate them to understand their impact and origins. Doing so allows us to determine alternatives that are more sustainable and respectful of the environment and to successfully make each piece of jewellery be more ethically responsible.

These materials are very wide ranging, but the most common ones are cotton, silk and leather, which are normally used to make bracelets or pendants.

Thanks to the fashion industry, it is possible to understand the damaging impact that these materials leave behind. In the case of cotton, we know that problems centre on monocultures, which leave farmers with no option to grow food; the application of powerful pesticides; and excessive consumption of water. For this reason, the best solution is to use organic cotton, which encourages the natural development of this raw material, respect for the environment and the promotion of fair trade.

The leather industry also produces a lot of pollution, a consequence mainly of the use of chemical compounds in the tanning process and in solvents and pigments. The problem arises when waste is dumped in to waters, which causes high pollution levels from substances such as chromium, zinc and lead.

4.28 | Cotton farming

Cotton is the most widely produced natural fibre in the world, but the excessive use of resources such as water and the application of agricultural chemicals in the growing process are causing serious problems such as water pollution. Biodiversity has also been affected by monocultures and the use of genetically modified seeds.

Photo: David Mark / pixabay.com

One of the alternative practices that reduces that impact is to apply ecological tanning processes in the form of vegetable tanning. It is a slower and somewhat more costly process, but it has a lower impact on the environment.

Another option are leathers described as "ecological" or "vegan," which do not contain any ingredients from animals and are made from cotton covered in recycled rubber or polyester.

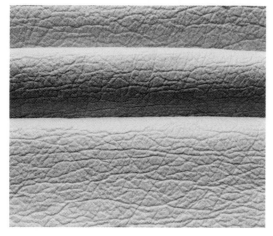

Dr. Carmen Hijosa, CEO of Ananas Anam Ltd., created Piñatex vegetable leather in 2013, a sustainable fabric produced from natural fibres extracted from pineapple. The whole process is carried out in accordance with a strict vision of sustainability that does not involve the use of excess water during cultivation or the application of fertilizers or toxins.

4.29 | PiñatexTM vegetable fabrics
Piñatex natural fabric by London-based firm Ananas Anam Ltd. The primary material for producing this fabric comes from pineapple plants grown in the Philippines.

Photo: Ananas Anam Ltd.

4.30 | Straps by Epaulettes
Epaulettes is the first brand focused exclusively on designing jewellery for women's shoulders. Its leather straps are tanned ecologically using natural processes and dyes.

Photo: Dani Gaya

Alternative materials

From wood to paper, a very wide range of materials can be used in jewellery nowadays, especially within the sector's more artistic branches.

It must be kept in mind that all materials that we use, and not just metals or gems, have an impact. For this reason, it is essential for us to ask ourselves where they come from and what they have left behind. Researching materials and production and extraction processes is now part of the aware entrepreneur or designer's job.

An example can be found in the use of wood. Certifications such as PEFC and FSC give consumers a guarantee that they are buying products from sustainably managed forests.

Researching the origins of and processes behind all materials to be used is now part of the job for entrepreneurs or designers who care about ethics and sustainability.

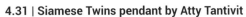

4.31 | Siamese Twins pendant by Atty Tantivit
Made from recycled wood scraps.
Photo: Panjapol Kulpapangkorn

4.32 | Brooche ID 0000000000003, from the series Silent Shout by Cherry Boonyapan and Kata Sangkhae

The collection Silent Shout is a collaboration between the artists Cherry Boonyapan y Kata Sangkhae. It consists of a rosary and brooches made of recycled brass. The colour used in some of the pieces is Sugar Artists Acrylics, a spray paint which doesn't contain petroleoum-derived ingredients.
Photo: Bo Piroonmas

4.31

4.32

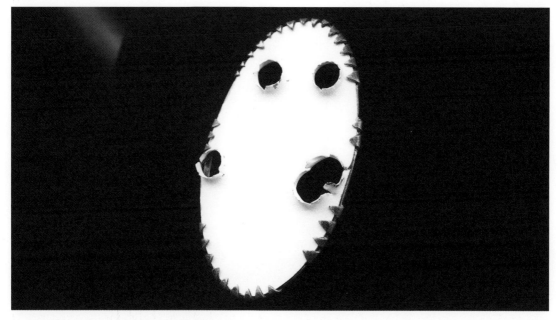

4.33 | Sugar Artists' Acrylic

Sugar Artists' Acrylic is a product from the company Ironlak. It is a spray paint that petroleum products have successfully been eliminated from through its formula combining water and alcohol with sugar cane. This makes it a much more responsible product in terms of health and the environment. Its high quality and range of colours have made it a high-performance, low-impact product.

Photo: Callie Marshall

Toby Pomeroy

4.34

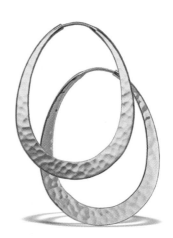

4.35

Toby Pomeroy is the creator and owner of a jewellery firm that shares his name. In creating its collections, the firm takes sustainability on board in order to improve the health, beauty and diversity of our planet and its peoples.
Toby's social and environmental engagement led him to change his conception of jewellery, and he was one of the first designers to demand certifications for recycled metals. He now works with conflict-free gems and diamonds and with Fairmined-certified sustainable recycled metals.

What exactly was the source of your motivation or ambition to start making sustainable jewellery?

I wanted to know that whatever I was doing as a designer-goldsmith left Earth a better place than it was at the moment. Not unlike the conscientious visitors to nature's wilderness who have as their creed *leave no trace*, my focus has been to foster a culture in the jewellery industry of taking care of the planet and those who live here, now and into the future.

4.34 | Toby Pomeroy
Photo: Basil Childers

4.35 | Oval Eclipse earrings by Toby Pomeroy
Made from 18k recycled EcoGold.
Photo: Michael Cuiccio

What was the first step for you to build up a sustainable way of thinking and making?

I was at first impacted by the deplorable environmental conditions surrounding the jewellery industry and declared to myself that I could no longer make jewellery if I wasn't doing everything possible to have my efforts increase awareness and inspire responsable actions in others, inside and outside the industry.

What kind of attitude should the jeweller have as a jewellery designer to create the ethical and be more environmental awareness of their own profession?

I'd say that if one wants to live a completely meaningful life they could do no better than to commit themselves to discovering their true purpose, their *raison d'etre*, and give themselves fully to it.

4.36 | Eclipse earrings and bracelet by Toby Pomeroy

Made from 18k recycled EcoGold and conflict-free diamonds.

Photo: Michael Jones

Toby Pomeroy

4.37

4.38

Is it a big challenge for you to discover a new step in a sustainable jewellery business?

Yes, in some ways it is a challenge. However, at the same time, I am confident that when we're passionate about something, are really committed to the fulfillment of something and alert to that possibility being fulfilled, we will discover the next door for us to open and step through.

4.37 | Earrings by Toby Pomeroy

Ginkgo earrings made from 18k recycled EcoGold and ethically sourced diamonds.

Photo: Michael Cuiccio

4.38 | Collection by Toby Pomeroy

Earrings and necklace made from 18k recycled EcoGold.

Photo: Michael Jones

How do you apply the sustainable way of thinking into the design process?

I believe it is of paramount importance that each of us is in touch with and anchored in what we're here for, the game we're playing that's bigger than our own survival, that inspires us and is worthy of devoting our life to.
When we are passionate about and connected to the reason for our existence, everything we do is an expression of that purpose: our relationships, our self-expression and our design. Because we're committed to fulfilling a purpose beyond our own narrow self-interest our lives themselves become a manifestation of sustainability.

What do you think about the future of sustainable jewellery?

I believe the future for the jewellery industry is very bright. As far as I can tell, nearly everyone who is entering the jewellery profession today is aware of the absolute need to have as an element of their expression a focus on sustainability.

As a culture we are increasingly aware that we've pushed ourselves close to an environmental point of no return and know that to have a future with a quality of life approaching that of preceding generations, we must act now and act consistently.

Can you give some advice to the new coming jewellery designers? Who want to create their own sustainable jewellery brand.

Much of what I would offer I've stated above. I would add the recommendation of trusting oneself, trusting that anything is possible and consistently taking bold action.

4.39 | Oasis necklace by Toby Pomeroy
Necklace made from discs made from EcoSilver and 14k EcoGold.
Photo: Michael Cuiccio

4.40 | Toby Pomeroy and Jon Rudolph
Toby Pomeroy with one of his sustainable metal suppliers, Jon Rudolph, at the Mammoth Tusk mine in the Yukon, Canada.
Photo: Brooke McLean

A&E Metals
www.aemetal.com.au

Alianza por la Minería Responsable
www.responsiblemines.org

Ananas Anam
www.ananas-anam.com

Atty Tantivit
www.attagallery.com

CanadaMark
www.canadamark.com

Cherry Boonyapan
www.cherryboonyapan.com

Columbia Gem House
www.columbiagemhouse.com

Cookson Gold
www.cooksongold.es

Diamond Foundry
www.diamondfoundry.com

Eapaulettes
www.epaulettes.es

Fair Trade Jewellery Co
www.ftjco.com

Fairmined
www.fairmined.org

Fairtrade Gold
www.fairgold.org

FSC
www.fsc.org

Gemfields
www.gemfields.co.uk

Hija de la Laguna documental
www.hijadelalaguna.pe

Hoover & Strong
www.hooverandstrong.com

Inspira Diamonds
www.inspiradiamonds.com

Kamoka Pearls
kamokapearls.com

Kata Sangkhae
www.katasangkhae.com

Kinross Gold Corporation
www.kinross.com

Majoral
www.majoral.com

Melville Fine Jewellery
www.melvillejewellery.com

Nineteen 48
www.nineteen48.com

Origin Australia
www.originaustralia.com

PEFC
www.pefc.es

Pure Grown Diamonds
www.puregrowndiamonds.com

Rapaport Fair Trade
www.rapaportfairtrade.com

Rio Tinto
www.riotinto.com

Ruby Fair
www.rubyfair.com

SCS Global Services
www.scsglobalservices.com

Soko
www.shopsoko.com

Stuller
www.stuller.com

Sugar Artists' Acrylic
sugarartistsacrylic.com

Sustainable Pearls
www.sustainablepearls.org

The Rock Hound
www.therockhound.com

Tiffany & Co.
www.tiffany.com

Toby Pomeroy
www.tobypomeroy.com

Umicore
www.umicore.com

United Precious Metals
www.unitedpmr.com

Vipa Design
www.vipadesigns.co.uk

5

PRODUCTION
PROCESSES

5.1 | The smelting process
The firm Made uses recycled brass
to make its piece.
Photo: Cedric Mungai

Understanding raw materials

A long chain of processes is required to be able to convert an idea for jewellery into a product. Giving a piece of jewellery its material form requires the use of various resources that must be adapted to the concept of sustainability established during the design phase. Research has to be carried out into how to reduce the impact of each of the steps needed.

Understanding how suppliers work, seeking out ethical guarantees and reducing the impact that certain production techniques have are key parts of making our activities as respectful and ethical as possible.

In the process of making a piece of jewellery, understanding the raw materials to be used plays a fundamental role, since this factor can alter the production phase owing to the characteristics of each of the materials.

When working with sustainable metals, processes such as microfusion can become more complicated when third parties are needed to complete production. Neither sustainable metals that are certified at the point of extraction nor 100% recycled metals can be mixed with other metals whose origins we are not sure about. If we do mix them, we will no longer be able to guarantee sustainability, and we will lose the right to use the certifications.

5.2 | Wedding rings by Bario Neal

The US firm Bario Neal uses Fairmined-certified sustainable gold.

As the photo shows, conducting audits and applying exhaustive controls to the metals used produces the right to use the Fairmined mark in each of the firm's pieces.

Photo: Bario Neal

Depending on the production levels, this can be a problem, especially when it comes to finding a suitable supplier that can work exclusively with the sustainable raw materials that it receives, without mixing them with other clients' materials.

When creating one-off pieces, using sustainable metals is a much simpler task, since microfusion is not required. The metal is worked directly as the piece is made by hand, and if no changes are made to the metal, we can continue to maintain a transparent supply chain with precisely traceable materials used and the respective certifications for them.

Ecological or 100% recycled metals cannot be mixed with other materials whose origins we are not aware of, as we cannot continue to guarantee traceability and sustainability.

Finding guarantees

It is important to be able to rely on certain guarantees. Establishing firm commercial ties with suitable suppliers is an important step in obtaining trustworthy assurances. Aside from the various existing certifications that guarantee the origins of metals, in the case of diamonds and coloured gems, we have to trust in the legitimacy of each provider.

To have assurances as to the sustainability of their products, designers have to seek these guarantees in relation to materials that, when used in a responsible production process, will make a general contribution to minimizing impacts.

A range of international organizations offer guarantees about different providers. Being a member of one of these also demonstrates each firm or designer's declaration of intentions and ethical policies.

Relevant organizations

Ethical Metalsmith was founded in 2004. Its objective is to spread and inform consumers and professionals about sustainable, responsible and ethical practices and initiatives related to the mining, extraction and sale of the majority of the raw materials used to make jewellery. Its website offers a wealth of information about suppliers of ethical raw materials and a list of firms and designers that deploy a sustainable approach to jewellery making.

Artisanal Gold Council (AGC) is a nonprofit organization based in Canada. It is centred on promoting environmentally responsible artisanal mining under decent working conditions. Its educational projects for mining communities located in Africa, Asia and South America focus on the reduction of the use of toxic agents such as mercury, management of waste and worker health and safety, so as to bring about international commercial partnerships.

The Alliance for Responsible Mining is a global initiative that seeks the sustainable development of small-scale and artisanal mining through a worldwide network of experts and supporters. Its commitment to social justice and environmental responsibility has led it to develop the Fairmined standard for gold and precious metals in order to transform the mining sector.

The Responsible Jewellery Council is a nonprofit organization and international certification body. It addresses issues related to human rights, labour rights, environmental impacts and mining practices, in pursuit of offering a transparent supply chain for the jewellery industry. This organization has over 900 members, and it encompasses all of the sector's activities, from mining companies to retailers. They are subject to independent audits that ensure responsible and ethical practices within diamond, gold and precious-metal trading.

Joyería Sostenible is a platform whose objective is to raise awareness of and provide information on bad practices within the jewellery industry for the benefit of all jewellery designers. Such bad practices may relate to the environment or to social ethics, and the organization promotes training and consulting solutions in order to implant new, more sustainable business models that provide ethical jewellery.

The Jeweltree Foundation works directly with mining communities and cooperatives located in countries in the developing world that run small-scale precious-metal, diamond and gem extraction operations. Its objective is to offer a transparent supply chain to suppliers and producers, to guarantee social and ethical responsibility through certification, and to help the aforementioned communities to receive fair returns through direct access to the international market.

Information about suppliers

Production processes for jewellery can vary greatly depending on the techniques used, and each process is made up of different stages. However, in spite of this, to apply sustainability within production processes, it is necessary to strictly follow the suggestions and decisions made when designing a given piece. For example, it is essential to have a very clear idea of the raw materials that will be used. For this reason, design and production must have the same goals, a task that is easier when working at a small scale or in a small studio.

But whether the maker is a craftsperson or a small business, within the production processes there are certain tasks that are often delegated, which entails collaborations and external suppliers.

There should be control over and guarantees about the ethical practices applied within the production processes delegated to external businesses.

We have to be sure about the way in which these suppliers—for example, smelters or platers—work. If their practices do not respect the environment, neither will yours, as your production will contribute to producing a negative impact.

5.3

The jewellery workshop

When working on an individual or artisanal basis, the majority of production processes are carried out in a single workshop, which simplifies the management of all the processes owing to the fact that the working team is very small. This makes it possible not only to control the raw materials used but also to manage all the waste generated over the production cycle.

It is important to control and correctly recycle pollutants such as acids, oxides and other chemical products used in a jewellery workshop. To give an example, residue left on work desks or in the filters of polishing machines has to be recovered and recycled.

5.4

5.3 - 5.4 | JEM's workshop

Through its website, JEM Jewellery Ethically Minded communicates the careful way in which it makes jewellery to its customers. Craftspeople's savoir-faire is undoubtedly a fundamental part of the ethical policies of each brand when ensuring a sustainable process from start to finish.

Photos: Ludovic Parisot

Beyond the environmental pollution that all these substances can cause, it is very important to implement certain safeguards in the workplace. It must be understood that the most activities carried out in the process of producing a jewellery piece leave traces of elements that are harmful to human health. These elements can be almost invisible, but it has been shown that numerous chemical agents are present within a jewellery workshop.

We can find toxic agents in the form of dust in the atmosphere that contains different harmful metals depending on if what is being made is real or imitation jewellery, as the metals used are different. In addition, the pastes used to polish jewellery contain silica, aluminium and iron trioxide particles.

Another way in which these chemical agents come about is as gases produced through the heating of acids or the processes of smelting and annealing metal. Because of this, it is essential to be able to rely on good facilities that offer workers safety guarantees—for example, good ventilation systems that reduce atmospheric contamination, or the use of suitable protection and clothing.

5.5 | Metal smelting in a jewellery workshop in Bangkok

Photo: Kittirat Sarndang

5.6 | Ute Decker's jewellery workshop

Photo: Ute Decker

Reducing toxic agents

A range of chemical products that are needed to make jewellery are often found in jewellery workshops. These products are highly toxic, and without appropriate handling and recycling, they may cause major pollution problems.

The best practice here is to reduce the use of these chemical products by turning to less toxic alternatives, thereby considerably reducing the impact on the environment.

For example, citric acid or solutions made of common salt and vinegar are effective alternatives for replacing the use of sulphuric acid, a toxic product that is commonly used in jewellery workshops. When diluted, it whitens silver and gold pieces following their exposure to flame in metal soldering or annealing processes.

These alternatives are very economical and biodegradable as well as easy to work with, but it must be kept in mind that there are also certain risks if gases resulting from heating them are inhaled. As a result, it is always necessary to take appropriate safety measures into account when working.

Deoxidizers with greater sustainability

Citric acid: Can easily be obtained in powdered form. As effective as sulphuric acid when diluted in water and after heating the solution.

Vinegar: By mixing white wine vinegar with iodized salt, it is possible to obtain a completely environmentally friendly deoxidizer. Once the solution is heated, the results are as good as those obtained through citric acid.

Innovation and traditional practices

From a sustainability point of view, returning to traditional practices and techniques is certainly one solution for working in a more respectful way. But it should not be forgotten that even by using these, it is possible to commit acts that destroy the environment. As a result, common sense must always be used, and we need to ask ourselves about the impact that they may have.

On the other hand, innovation can also contribute major solutions for sustainable practices.

The use of 3D design, prototyping and printing offers great possibilities in terms of minimizing the use of resources such as the metals required to produce a prototype. Printing with wax allows us to save time and money, and at the same time it cuts down on the number of hours spent in the workshop handling chemical products and consuming electricity and gas.

5.7

5.8

5.7 | Artisanal process

Designer María Goti combines artisanal techniques and 3D design depending on the language of each piece. Regardless of the technique, she always applies the same ethics and sustainability criteria, extracting maximum efficiency in each case.

Photo: Joaquín González

5.8 | Jewellery by María Goti designed using 3D

As we will see later on, the use of 3D design can also be a sales strategy, as it reduces stock surpluses and removes the need to produce large numbers of pieces to show off a collection. Instead, an on-demand sales model can be used.

Innovation offers us tools that can be used very effectively to contribute to sustainable development in the production process by making that process more agile and less polluting.

The use of technology can also offer incredible results at the same time as allowing ethical aspects to be taken into account. This is the case of The Rock Hound and the firm's Chromanteq collection.

The starting point for this collection is ethically sourced gems. Based on the shape and dimensions of the gems, the jewellery pieces are made using 3D applications.

This means that each piece is unique and makes more effective use of all its resources, since the design is adapted to the stone chosen. Another technology that is a surprising aspect of this collection is a nanoceramic coating. This technique covers the metal used in the jewellery pieces, giving them a colour range that makes them unique. It should be added that the metal used to make these pieces is 100% recycled gold.

5.9 | Earrings from the Chromanteq collection by The Rock Hound

18k white gold earrings with an orange and blue nanoceramic coating, with tourmaline from Namibia and orange garnet from Nigeria.

Photo: AC Cooper

5.10 | Ring from the Chromanteq collection by The Rock Hound

9k pink gold ring coated in pink nanoceramics and 2.74ct spinel from Myanmar.

Photo: AC Cooper

Local production

As has already been explained, because of globalization, nowadays it is very simple and not particularly costly to carry out offshore production, even if this is only for part of the production process. Thanks to free trade and the Internet, it is very easy to contract for services in faraway countries where labour is cheaper—and where environmental regulations, sadly, may be more poorly enforced.

In this case, making sure that our practices do not harm the environment or are socially unethical is a much more difficult task due to distances and a lack of transparency. The most advisable thing to do would be to visit the country of origin to find out about its working conditions and what its regulations and measures achieve in terms of the environment. After examining different offers, it will likely be the case that the cheapest option will not be the most sustainable one.

5.11 | Earrings from the Planetas collection by Majoral made from Fairmined gold

In spite of the fact that it attends fairs across the world and has an international presence, Majoral continues to use a local production process, in which all details are attended to in its workshop located on the island of Formentera, in Spain.

Photo: Martin Azúa

5.12 | Ring made from Fairtrade gold and conflict-free gems by Melville

Each piece produced by Melville is hand-made by expert craftspeople at its workshops in Hong Kong.

Photo: © Melville Fine Jewellery

One way of solving or reducing this problem is to search for external collaborators or partners who are based nearby. This stimulates the local economy and enhances safety, control over processes and transparency. As for the sustainability levels of third parties, as we have seen, we will always be indirectly responsible for any of their bad practices, since they are part of the production chain for the product that we seek to sell.

5.13 - 5.14 | Necklace, earrings, bracelet, rings and brooch from the Respira collection by Marta Blanco in collaboration with Koeatania

Local projects such as Koetania in Barcelona reveal high levels of support for local suppliers on the jeweller's doorstep. Sustainability is part of its philosophy (which implies to not waste materials and resources, to be transparent and to have close relations with its customers), and it works with recycled metals and certifications such as Fairmined.

Photo: Fernando Gómez

Positive offshoring

A contrasting approach to local products is offshoring of production to developing countries, though not with the objective of making a return at any cost by taking advantage of the scarcity of regulations in those states. The idea is to offer opportunities to individuals and collectives that may have great potential based on craftsmanship but few options for selling their products or services efficiently.

Offshoring production in a positive way allows us to help marginalized collectives to experience economic development.

Various brands operate in this way, and they additionally make use of local raw materials, most of which are recycled. Through taking this approach, their contribution to sustainability is not focused on the social level alone.

A clear example of such practices is provided by the British firm Made, which produces all of its jewellery and accessories in collaboration with different communities in Kenya. Through doing so, it promotes local craftsmanship in terms of beauty and design. Its objective is to increase economic and social development through honest and transparent practices that make positive change possible. Each of its pieces is made by hand and with materials with recycled origins, which also promotes responsible recycling.

5.15

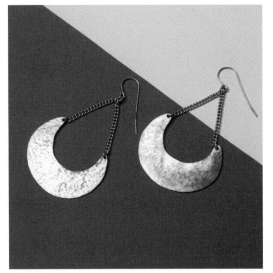

5.16

Made has been very effective in communicating its values and the craft quality of its pieces, which are made by hand in its workshops in Kenya. As a result, it has been involved in special collaborations with prestigious firms such as Tommy Hilfiger, Louis Vuitton, Stefanel and Top Shop.

5.15 | Earrings by Made

All jewellery by Made is produced by hand from recycled brass by Kenyan craftspeople.

Photo: Marga Berndich

5.16 | Craftspeople in Kenya working for Made

Photo: Cedric Mungai

5.17 | Shoulder bag Keepall 45 by Louis Vuitton

Bag produced in collaboration with the fairtrade brand Edun for the campaign Core Values. The bag includes a keyring/charm created by Made with the inscription Every journey began in Africa, handmade by Kenyan craftspeople.

Photo: © Louis Vuitton Malletier

Johanna Mejía

5.18

5.19

Johanna Mejía is the cofounder of jewellery firm Amalena, which takes sustainability principles from the fashion world and applies them to jewellery. Over its creation process, Amalena seeks to combat the complex problems related to illegal mining in Colombia. It offers visibility to the responsible miners that it works with, and it encourages the added value of craftsmanship.

5.18 | Johanna Mejía
Cofounder of Amalena.
Photo: Alexander Rieser

5.19 | Gaitana earrings by Amalena
Hand made from 18k EcoGold.
Photo: Alexander Rieser

How did the Amalena project come about?

Amalena was the result of my master's thesis, for which I studied artisanal and small-scale mining. I saw for myself the complex problems related to precious metals and their harmful impact on both people and the environment.

The conclusion was that, aside from the importance of promoting artisanal mining that is carried out responsibly, to have a greater impact in communities of this kind and to create shared value, it was necessary to also involve other vulnerable agents. This is how the link between gold from responsible sources and the production of jewellery by local craftswomen became stronger and brought about what is now my brand, Amalena.

5.20

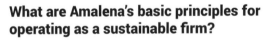

5.21

What are Amalena's basic principles for operating as a sustainable firm?

We follow three fundamental principles. Through the Fair Mine principle, we are committed to supporting artisanal and small-scale miners that carry out their activities in a sustainable manner. The principle of Fair Trade provides us with the parameters for fair working conditions and fair remuneration for both our miners and our craftspeople, and also for our company to follow strict guidelines in terms of ethics and social responsibility.

The last principle, Fair Price, is related to our social enterprise philosophy, through which we seek solutions to social and environmental problems and try to improve the living conditions of the vulnerable populations where we work.

5.20 | Sua earrings by Amalena

Produced by hand by craftswomen from La Llanada in Colombia, and made from 18k ecological gold.

Photo: Alexander Rieser

5.21 | Workshop in La Llanada where Amalena's craftswomen work

Photo: Alexander Rieser

Johanna Mejía

5.23

5.22

Who are Amalena's customers?

Our customers are people who take an interest in social and environmental matters. They understand the power that they have as consumers, and they are aware when they make buying decisions. They know that by choosing products that contribute to solving different problems, they do their little bit to make the world a better and fairer place for all of us.

5.22 | Butterfly necklace by Amalena

Hand made from 18k ecological gold by craftswomen from La Llanada. Neither mercury nor cyanide is used in the process of extracting the metal.

Photo: Alexander Rieser

What is it like to work with small communities of craftswomen?

It's a challenge, as these communities are isolated from big cities. Reaching them is difficult, and this is even more of a problem when you undertake a sustainable jewellery project like Amalena. What makes facing all of these challenges worth it is being able to have a direct impact on mining communities and work together in this process with the agents involved in creating our jewellery, from the miners who extract the gold to our metalsmiths, who work this precious metal to create our pieces. Hands and hearts join together to preserve the environment and cultural traditions through our jewellery.

5.24

What advice would you offer to jewellery students who wish to go about setting up a responsible jewellery firm?

First of all, they should be well informed. It is important to have a clear action plan and to know about the different forms of responsible jewellery. The key is to understand your brand and what it represents, and also to have a commercial strategy that allows you to successfully tell your story in a coherent way so that potential customers appreciate not just the aesthetic aspects of your pieces but also the added value that comes from creating them in a responsible way.

In your view, what difficulties might people encounter?

The main difficulty often relates to how to communicate the brand's concept. It is important to focus on the essentials. To begin with, you can't overwhelm the customer with information, though this does not mean that the jeweller's knowledge has to be superficial. There are always demanding customers who want to know more, and it is important to have answers for them.

In addition, the jeweller's approach to aesthetics cannot be sacrificed. The jeweller has to find materials that can be moulded to create the envisaged piece. This is a major challenge, as it's not easy to find responsible or sustainable materials, and this is why responsible jewellers need to be as much artists as they are creators when it comes to producing their work. This encompasses the materials, packaging and all the steps in between the two.

5.23 | Craftswomen who work with Amalena

A craftswoman using a tray and gravitational methods to separate gold from impurities without using mercury or cyanide. From very near to the mine, the craftswomen use this metal to produce jewellery.

Photo: Alexander Rieser

5.24 | Quilla earrings by Amalena

Hand made from 18k EcoGold.

Photo: Alexander Rieser

Alliance for Responsible Mining
www.responsiblemines.org

Amalena
www.amalena.es

Artisanal Gold Council
www.artisanalgold.org

Bario Neal
bario-neal.com

Edun
edun.com

Ethical Metalsmiths
www.ethicalmetalsmiths.org

JEM Jewellery Ethical Minded
www.jem-paris.com

Joyería Sostenible
www.joyeriasostenible.com

Koetania
www.koetania.com

Louis Vuitton
www.louisvuitton.com

Made
www.made.uk.com

Majoral
www.majoral.com

María Goti
mariagoti.es

Marta Blanco
www.marutadas.com

Melville Fine Jewellery
www.melvillejewellery.com

Responsible Jewellery Council
www.responsiblejewellery.com

The Jeweltree Foundation
www.jeweltreefoundation.org

The Rock Hound
www.therockhound.com

Ute Decker
utedecker.com

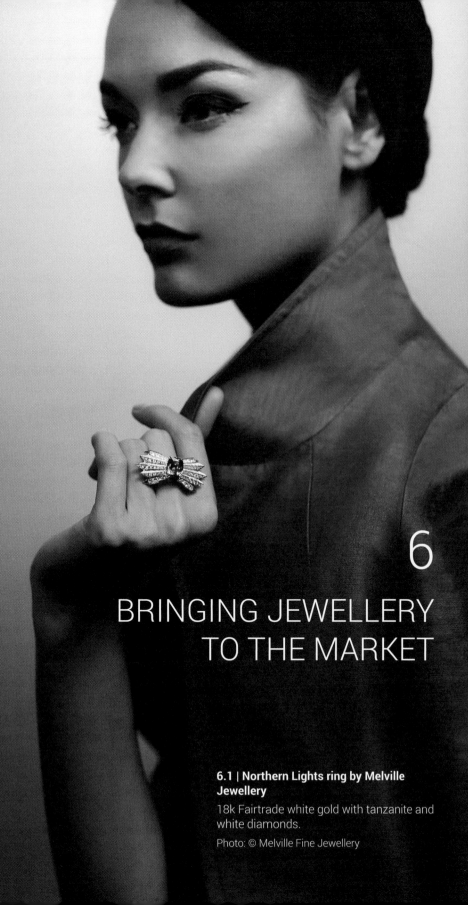

6

BRINGING JEWELLERY TO THE MARKET

6.1 | Northern Lights ring by Melville Jewellery

18k Fairtrade white gold with tanzanite and white diamonds.

Photo: © Melville Fine Jewellery

As we have seen prior to this point, the concept of sustainability is something that has repercussions on each of the phases involved in jewellery making, from raw materials to production. But we will also see that bringing jewellery to the market, which encompasses sales, distribution and packaging, can also be changed by adapting to more ethical and responsible values.

On-demand production

There are various ways to manage stock in a more responsible and effective way when the time comes to bring a jewellery collection to the market. Depending on the characteristics of each firm, different concepts and ways of working can be adapted so that the resources that we may use are not wasted.

One of the problems that we might encounter following a selling season is surplus stock. At first sight, this situation does not seem too complicated, since in the jewellery sector precious metals and gems can be recycled easily for reuse in making new pieces and collections.

But if we want to do things with awareness, we should also keep in mind that even if we can recycle all of our surplus stock, in addition to the time that we invested in making the piece, energy was also consumed—for example, gas (in smelting or assembly processes) and electricity (through the use of polishers, ultrasounds, work lamps and so forth). Even if all the materials are recycled to make a new piece of jewellery, none of this energy consumption can be recovered, which means that energy has been squandered and that a certain amount of pollution has been created.

It can be difficult to estimate required stock levels, but thanks to new technologies such as the Internet and 3D design, there are online stores that allow users to choose their pieces of jewellery before they are made, which means they can be produced on an on-demand basis. Firms such as James Allen are a clear example of this kind of sales strategy.

Opting for a slower, to-order form of artisanal production also resolves the problem of surplus stock. It is important to clearly communicate delivery time scales to the customer. To produce sustainably, these may be longer than usual.

Jewellery commissions

Craftspeople have always offered their clients the possibility to commission a piece of jewellery. Aside from the market for wedding-related jewellery, where commissions are common, this type of service by firms or designers is a way of making the most out of all the resources invested in the piece, as from the outset there is a buyer for it.

As a result, it is important to have customers who value exclusivity and understand the cost involved in a commissioned design.

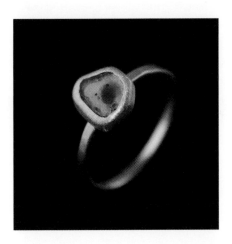

6.2 | 14k Ring made from recycled gold with an uncut sapphire from Montana by VK Designs

Designer Valerie Kasinskas specializes in offering her customers completely personalized jewellery pieces. Her customers can even provide the materials in the form of old pieces of jewellery that they have perhaps inherited. These old pieces are transformed into a new jewellery product.

Photo: Valerie Kasinskas

Redesigning

Redesigning a piece of jewellery, or giving customers the option of providing new pieces to be used as raw materials in the creation of a new piece, is a sustainable manufacturing method and a way of making consumers aware of recycling and conservation practices. It also works as a strategy for boosting sales, since customers' investments in order to obtain new jewellery pieces will be much lower.

6.3 | Collection of rings made from recycled gold and conflict-free diamonds by April Doubleday

On her website, designer April Doubleday's customers can provide an old piece of jewellery whose metal will be reused to make any of the pieces offered by the firm in its catalogue.

Photo: Nick Clarke

One-off pieces

Designing one-off pieces is another way of getting maximum use from resources. Normally, one-off pieces are found in high jewellery and can be fairly exclusive.

There are many firms that, in addition to the collections that they offer, also do a line of one-off pieces. Martalia is one such firm. In addition, there are also firms and designers like As Above So Below that focus exclusively on creating one-off pieces.

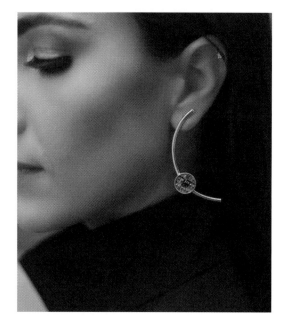

6.4 | Earrings from the collection Conexiones by Martalia

Ring designed by Estela Guitart and made from 18k Fairmined gold and tourmalines.

Photo: Cristina Gomis

6.5 | Ring by Anna Moltke-Huitfeldt made from 18k Green Gold free from chemical use at extraction, with keshi pearl cultivated in the Andaman Sea

Anna Moltke-Huitfeldt was the first metalsmith in Denmark to obtain the Fairmined and Fairtrade certifications for ethically sourced metals. Many of the jewellery pieces that she makes are one-offs.

Photo: Anna Moltke-Huitfeldt

To make sustainable jewellery using the approach of producing one-off pieces, the raw materials used must comply with certain requirements. This is the case for metals that are recycled or certified under licence, as well as for ethically sourced gems.

6.7 | Ring made from 18k Fairmined gold with black river tourmaline by As Above So Below

As Above So Below designer Azalea Lee creates talismanic pieces. The rarity and qualities of her gems make each piece unique, though they are always produced ethically and sustainably.

Photo: As Above So Below

6.6 | Pendant by As Above So Below

Made from 18 k gold with tourmaline from Nigeria and natural black tourmalines.

Photo: As Above So Below

Solutions that offer greater sustainability

When we think about what things have a highly damaging impact on the planet's ecosystem, one type of item that ought to come to mind is the packaging that accompanies practically every product that we consume. Packaging is produced by virtually all sectors, and its effect is excessive because it has a short life cycle. Most of the time its job is to protect and transport products— jewellery, in our case—and to keep them in optimum condition. That is, the packaging is made for the journey between store and home and little else.

One of the problems that we may encounter is that jewellery packaging requires a certain presence, as jewellery is often a luxury item. This factor often means having to use an excess of resources to make the packaging, which usually also entails the use of nonrenewable raw materials or processes that are very costly and polluting.

It seems contradictory to have jewellery that is sustainable in packaging that is not.

6.8 | The iconic Blue Box® by Tiffany & Co

With the goal of reducing its environmental footprint, Tiffany & Co. made its iconic packaging environmentally friendly by turning to paper from responsibly managed forests and using recycled paper.

Photo: © Tiffany & Co.

6.9 | PEFC certification

PEFC-certified products such as wood, paper and cork give consumers a guarantee that they are buying products that come from sustainably managed forests. By choosing PEFC, purchasers can help to combat illegal logging.

The packaging used by jewellery firms says a lot, as its design allows us to communicate the firm's values and essence. Because packaging is an important element in the sale of jewellery, we must also take note of the impact that it has on the environment, as many materials that are regularly used may not fulfil sustainability criteria. The visual link between a product and its packaging is very important, since the first information that the customer obtains is from the container and not its content, which makes it unthinkable to offer a product that is sustainable in packaging that is not.

6.10 - 6.11 | Packaging for Majoral designed by Martin Azúa

Majoral's packaging is made using a simple unvarnished pine frame that is coated in white cotton canvas. It closes with strips made from the same material. It asserts an honest and restrained luxury in which simple and natural materials play the leading role.

Photo: Martin Azúa

6.12 | Materials used in making Coral Covey's packaging

Coral Covey uses recycled materials to make its packaging.

Photo: Laura Deakin

For this reason, it is very important for sustainable jewellery firms to have ethical packaging that protects the environment—or at least damages it as little as possible—as a collateral effect to its main function. Eco philosophy must be reflected in packaging that has a pleasing look and an original design but that above all demonstrates respect for the environment.

We cannot sell sustainable jewellery in a plastic box made from petroleum derivatives. Doing so would be completely contradictory, and the consumer would be receiving mixed messages.

There are many possibilities when it comes to finding packaging companies that work with either recycled or completely recyclable paper or cardboard. One example is Self Packaging (www.selfpackaging.com), a company that provides information on its sustainability certifications.

Another company that often works with a range of sustainable jewellery firms— for example, Coral Covey—is Tiny Box Company (www.tinyboxcompany.co.uk), which exclusively employs recycled materials. Among the advantages offered by these companies' services are the option of personalizing packaging, the possibility of placing orders through their websites and the fact that, in many cases, it is not necessary to place a minimum order.

Innovative contributions

The conclusion that we might arrive at is that the packaging used by an ethical and sustainable jewellery firm must also respect the environment and convey the same values as the firm's jewellery. It must additionally be original and perform a protective function. As a result, it is necessary to use sustainable materials, or even to offer the possibility of extending the packaging's useful life. Therefore, some imagination is required to help the consumer give it another use.

One example of a major innovation of this type comes from The Rock Hound, which uses innovative packaging made from fish leather. This material is based on a subproduct from the fishing industry that has no other use. It is saved and turned into highly exotic leather that gives the packaging added value. The leather is tanned by an Icelandic company using renewable geothermal energy.

Delivery packaging

In addition to the packaging in which the jewellery is presented, it is also necessary to take into account the type of packaging used to deliver orders to customers and points of sale. Once again, sustainability must be a factor in the form of using parcels and boxes made with materials that are recycled or sourced from forests managed by a certification system.

As we will see, many package-delivery companies use green packaging of this kind.

6.13 | Packaging by The Rock Hound

The Rock Hound uses fish leather sourced from the fishing industry, which has no other use for the raw material used to make the leather. Fish skin is recovered and tanned through an environmentally friendly process that turns it into an exotic leather that the firm uses to create added value.

Photo: AC Cooper

Logistics

In order to be able to reduce our carbon footprint as much as possible, we need to choose the least polluting means of transport, or ones that are involved in environmental offsetting programmes. There are different companies in both Europe and the Americas that, aware of the severe impact that transportation has, specialize in goods-delivery services that counteract that impact. In the case of FedEx, its EarthSmart programme is focused on applying comprehensive solutions that help to reduce its footprint—for example, using hybrid and electric vehicles, optimizing its use of resources and fuel, and using sustainable packaging.

Employing similar strategies, UPS has a Carbon Neutral programme, a service that any user can choose when making a delivery and that calculates the carbon dioxide emissions that will occur up until the moment of the package's arrival at its destination. UPS commits to subsequently undertaking offsetting activities in the form of various reforesting, waste-water treatment and other projects.

6.14 | | FedEx Express delivery package
The EarthSmart programme offers delivery boxes and packages made from recycled cardboard and paper.
Photo: © FedEx

Even if we turn to nearby suppliers and produce locally, the possibility of selling online means that there really are no borders. Online selling entails making national and international deliveries, and to make these it is better to seek out alternatives that are more efficient in terms of pollution and to choose ground transportation whenever possible, even if doing so means that delivery will be slower. If our deliveries are for within our city, we can use environmentally friendly transportation such as bicycles. Some delivery companies offer this method as part of their services.

It is important to find out about the green and CO$_2$-offsetting programmes offered by different courier and haulage firms.

Online commerce

Using digital platforms such as websites for communications strategies and online sales is an absolute necessity. Although this is a purely digital format, it requires the use of Web hosts that store all of the content. These servers have a physical location. The practices of Web hosts, whether they relate to waste handling or energy consumption, can contribute to unsustainable practices.

There are many green Web hosting services whose philosophy is to reduce their carbon footprint by using renewable and efficient energy or by investing in offsetting programmes.

www.greenwebhost.net
asmallorange.com
www.ecowebhosting.co.uk

6.15 | FedEx delivery van

FedEx has fleets of electric and hybrid vehicles in different European and North American cities as part of its EarthSmart programme.

Photo: © FedEx

Laura Deakin

Australian designer Laura Deakin, who founded jewellery firm Coral Covey in 2013, has opted to produce ethically through the use of recycled metals. Through the company Polarstern, she is able to power her Munich workshop with clean and renewable energy. Offering packaging made with recycled materials and incorporating carbon offsetting programmes in her deliveries have contributed to her being able to offer ethical jewellery that makes a difference in terms of environmental impact.

When did you start to have an interest in sustainable jewellery?

As a child my grandmother taught me how important it was to care for my environment, and since then I have always attempted to live my life in the most sustainable way. When I started my own jewellery line, Coral Covey Jewellery, in 2013, it felt like the only way to do it would be fairly, sustainably and mindfully.

6.16 | Laura Deakin

This Australian designer has established herself in Munich, Germany, where she has a workshop-studio.

Photo: Alan Thompson

6.17 | Vivi's Golden Edelweiss earrings by Coral Covey

Made with recycled silver with 24k gold plating.

Photo: Laura Deakin

How do you go about using green energy such as 100% renewable gas and electricity in the studio?

In Munich there are several energy providers who offer renewable electricity and gas, but Polarstern (www.polarstern-energie.de), I felt, was the best option on the market. They are a young company who is not only committed to providing legitimately green power; they are also using this knowhow in developing nations such as Cambodia (www.polarstern-energie.de/weltweit). In the Coral Covey studio we try to minimize our overall power use by using energy-saving bulbs, only heating rooms that are in use and turning off all power to the studio when we leave at night.

How do you spread awareness about making sustainable jewellery to the customer?

This has been difficult, but slowly the message is getting out. We take a big interest in current articles, media and film that concentrate on the issues related to the mining of buried precious metals because it's such a destructive process, both environmentally and socially. Customers can find a lot of information on our website and via all our social media. In an age where you can swipe past an image without reading any content, it's sometimes hard to grab a viewer's eye, but more people are taking an interest in sustainable living and this has meant a lot more people seek out locally made, fair and sustainable items.

6.18 | Karen's Love Heart pendant by Coral Covey
Pendant made with 100% recycled silver, to which pink gold plating has been applied.
Photo: Laura Deakin

Laura Deakin

6.19

How do your costumers react once they know your products are made out of 100% recycled materials?

This is a fun part! We love explaining this aspect of Coral Covey to our customers and it is always received with such enthusiasm. Some customers come to us because they saw and liked the jewellery and didn't realise we were a fair and sustainable company, so when they find out how we are using only recycled silver and gold and not supporting the mining of new materials it is an added bonus. Other customers come to us because the know we are using reclaimed and recycled materials and it's a pleasure to explain how and why we do this.

Which difficulties or problems have you found in the process of making your jewellery sustainable?

There are extra costs involved in sourcing sustainable and/or natural materials, so this is sometimes irritating, but I think the hardest thing has been to get the message out about how our jewellery differs from something made by the thousand in a developing nation. We take pride in each piece being not only sustainably made, but also handmade. By designing each piece and develop the techniques involved in reproducing it and this requires time and a lot of love.

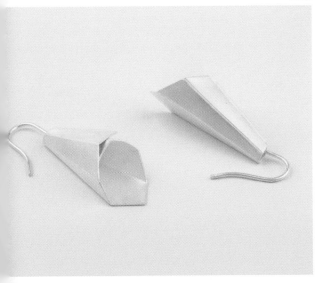

Can you give some advice to the new beginner jeweller who would love to start the sustainable jewellery business?

At the beginning it's essential to pay attention to detail. Coral Covey began using recycled silver and gold, then sourced a local casting company to work with, then came all the other decisions from powering the workshop to using recycled materials for our packaging. Change the things you can to develop a local and sustainable company/ workshop and all the other things will follow.

6.19 - 6.20 | Mel's Folded Spaces earrings by Coral Covey

Made from 100% recycled silver.

Photo: Laura Deakin

6.21 | Karen's Golden Heart earrings by Coral Covey

Made from recycled silver with 24k gold plating. The packaging and other corporate elements such as the business cards are made from sustainable and recycled materials.

Photo: Laura Deakin

Anna Moltke-Huitfeldt
www.moltke-huitfeldt.com

April Doubleday
www.aprildoubleday.com

As Above So Below
www.jdljewellery.co.uk/as-above-so-below

Coral Covey
coralcovey.com

EarthSmart de FedEX
www.fedex.com/ru_english/about/sustainability/earthsmart.html

James Allen
www.jamesallen.com

Majoral
www.majoral.com

Martalia
www.martalia.com

Martin Azúa
www.martinazua.com

Melville Fine Jewellery
www.melvillejewellery.com

PEFC
www.pefc.org

Self Packaging
www.selfpackaging.com

The Rock Hound
www.therockhound.com

Tiffany & Co.
www.tiffany.com

Tiny Box Company
www.tinyboxcompany.co.uk

UPS Carbon Neutral
www.carbonneutral.ups.com

VK Designs
www.valkasinskas.com

CREATING SUSTAINABILITY STRATEGIES

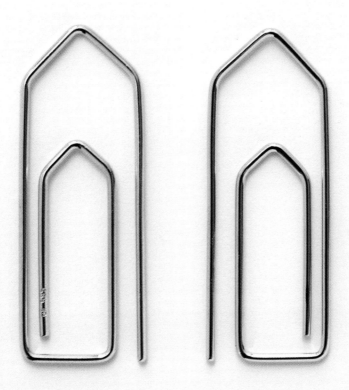

7.1 | Clip-on earrings by Goldfingers
Made from 18k Fairmined gold.
Photo: Kenneth Øksnebjerg

The path towards change

As we have seen throughout this book, there are various problems related to jewellery that severely affect both the environment and social ethics. If we are conscious of these, we will either be part of the problem or part of the solution depending on which side of the fence we choose to place ourselves.

It is within a jewellery firm or designer's grasp to offer jewellery that is ethical in terms of the subjects that we have considered here. And it is down to consumers to seek more information when making a purchase in order to find out about the impact of each product that we consume.

Getting a sustainable jewellery firm off the ground is a very personal decision that must be taken with complete conviction about the values and principles that this commitment entails. Through choosing this path, we can offer complete transparency and honesty about our practices.

If we truly want to execute this option correctly, we need to make extra efforts, first in terms of time and the search for information, and then possibly in economic terms.

Making the change is unquestionably not an easy one. It requires long-term commitment that has to become part of the company's philosophy, not just in terms of the objective to be achieved but also in terms of the path to be travelled, innovating over time and applying new formulas that allow sustainability to be improved.

7.2 | Ring made from 18k recycled gold and ethically sourced uncut diamond by Fluid Jewellery

The ethical principles held by Caelen Ellis, founder of the jewellery firm Fluid Jewellery, do not just focus on the ethical raw materials that he uses. He also has a programme through which he allocates 5% of his sales to different causes.

Photo: Caelen Ellis

Requirements

Any action will entail certain requirements that have to be met, and for our jewellery firm to go down the path of sustainability, it is necessary for us to understand certain things that will turn our intentions into a viable project.

If we decide to conduct our business ethically, we need to understand the scope of the harmful impact that is being produced, and find out what solutions and alternatives are available.

Through doing so, we can carry out a specific evaluation of the tangible and intangible needs of a strategy designed to integrate sustainability into our business.

Finally, it is essential to plan for the long term. Each step taken to integrate sustainable aspects will be slow. As we have seen already, it is a question of swimming against the tide, something that slows things down in comparison to what happens when starting a conventional project.

Patience and a vision for the future are unfailing allies in being able to formulate a realistic programme that will allow our strategy to succeed. Each ethical supplier found, each certification or licence acquired, and each key partnership established will be an achievement that will create personal and professional satisfaction and clear the path for us to keep moving forward and improving each day.

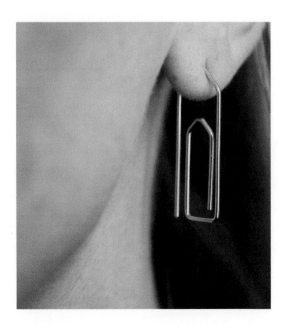

7.3 | Clip earrings made from 18k Fairtrade gold by Goldfingers

Janne K. Hansen and Karl Ejnar Nybo are the creatives behind Copenhagen-based firm and gallery Goldfingers. Its pieces are made by hand using Fairtrade metals.

Photo: Kenneth Øksnebjerg

An expanding market

It is becoming increasingly clear that ecology is a current issue in many sectors and that it poses unavoidable questions. This creates a business opportunity, as demand for products that meet sustainability standards is rising.

As was said in the first chapter of this book, consumers who have developed an empathy towards the products that they buy will continue to become more numerous. This offers the possibility of operating in an emerging market, and it is vital for all the firms and designers within it to have sustainability programmes for their practices.

On the other hand, this clear tendency can cause a certain amount of confusion in other, more poorly informed customers, who may be pushed to buy products that proclaim that they are sustainable but in fact are not. As we will see later on, the key thing is not just to communicate our activities, but also to inform consumers so that they understand the added value that a jewellery piece designed in accordance with strictly ethical criteria has.

7.4 | Ring from the Spinel collection by Tura Sugden made from 18k recycled gold with natural spinels

North American designer Tura Sugden makes her pieces with Fairmined-certified sustainable gold, recycled metals and ethically sourced gems.

Photo: Marina George

Greenwashing

In the interview contained in this chapter, Joan Gomis, the head of Misui, is asked what advice he would offer to designers interested in adopting sustainable practices. In his answer, he talks about avoiding communications activities about green initiatives when no solution is really being provided to the problems described throughout this book.

Communication of this kind may be intentional and done because of the new business opportunities that the market has in its sights, but it may also come from well-intentioned designers who, because they do not fully understand what the priority issues are, focus on solving problems through secondary activities. This leads—albeit unintentionally—to engaging in greenwashing practices. Greenwashing is a term that describes the use of misleading green marketing to make people believe that particular products or policies connected to a company are appropriate from an environmental point of view.

Nor should we mix up an enthusiasm for wanting to offer sustainable solutions with talking about offering them when we are in fact not. We need to have sustainable practices that do provide real solutions. If we wish to go down the path of sustainability, we must do so in a rigorous and honest way and while offering guarantees. If we do not do this, rather than providing solutions, we will worsen the situation, as consumers will end up being unable to distinguish between proper activities and what may just be good intentions or a commercial strategy.

To avoid slipping up in this way, it is very important for the jewellery firm to establish a strategy for incorporating sustainability, first of all by identifying what are the most acute issues on which we will need to focus to provide solutions, and then gradually disseminating those same values in other areas that are also necessary for the firm in undertaking its activities.

7.5 | Areas in which to apply a sustainable strategy within a jewellery firm

**DESIGN
RAW MATERIALS
PRODUCTION
RECYCLING**

**PACKAGING
SHIPPING
INSTALLATIONS**

**SOCIAL ACTIONS
DONATIONS**

First steps

Once we have identified the weakest points concerning sustainability in the supply chain, it is necessary to turn to applying solutions that are effective and do not simply paper over the cracks.

One significant risk factor in jewellery is the raw materials linked to the product, especially when there is no certainty as to their origins or a lack of any kind of guarantee. If we have not yet resolved this part of the supply chain, it is the first area that we need to focus our efforts on.

As we saw in Chapter 4, aside from understanding the problems that lie behind every gram of gold, silver or platinum, and apart from the cruelty and injustice that may be associated with any precious metal, there are also different solutions that exist to make an ethical contribution through more sustainable raw materials.

To acquire Fairtrade or Fairmined licences, we must undertake certain procedures that can be both complex and costly to begin with. Depending on how big the designer's business is, these may be the first obstacle we encounter.

7.6 | Red, yellow and white teardrop earrings made from 18k Fairtrade gold by Amanda Li Hope.

British designer Amanda Li Hope has been using Fairtrade gold since 2011. She was one of the first 20 metalsmiths in the world to use the Fairtrade certification for gold. The diamonds and coloured stones are ethically sourced.

Photo: Amanda Li Hope

Another option for decreasing the use of mined raw materials is the possible use of recycled metals. If we take this option, it is necessary to turn to suppliers that guarantee via certifications the traceability of the metals, which will need to be 100% recycled. This allows complete transparency as to the product's sustainability to be offered and real solutions to be provided. If only a low percentage of recycled metal has been used, we will be feeding the problem at its roots.

7.7 | Recycled silver and pink gold pendant by Bario Neal

Bario Neal uses a range of solutions— for example, 100% recycled metals and Fairmined certification—to address the impact of conventional raw materials.

Photo: Bario Neal

7.7

7.8 | Engagement ring made from 18k Fairmined white gold and diamonds by Ana González

Colombian designer Ana González was one of the pioneers in using Fairmined-certified gold.

Photo: Ana González

7.9 | Handmade bracelet made from Fairmined .925 silver and obsidian from Sissai's Kené collection

In August 2016, Sissai acquired a Fairmined licence, which allows the firm to support the sustainable development of small-scale mining. This status has made Sissai the first Peruvian jewellery firm to work with certified sustainable metals such as Fairmined gold and silver.

Photo: Sissai Jewelry

7.8

Creating key partnerships

As we have seen, production and its different processes also have to be synchronized so that it is possible for each jewellery piece to be sustainable. If production is limited and is dependent on microfusion techniques provided by third parties, the sustainable metals will end up being mixed with other clients' metals, which will rule out the right to use any kind of certification owing to the impossibility of demonstrating the metal's traceability and origin.

This is something that ought to be kept in mind when formulating a strategy, as there can be direct repercussions on the selection of suppliers or on the establishment of key partnerships that can eliminate the problem from our production chain.

In the case of new designers, beginning a sustainable jewellery project can initially prove to be difficult. The problem lies in the sourcing of more sustainable raw materials and in the accompanying bureaucracy and costs arising from certifications and licences. Moreover, as we have seen, production processes may run into initial difficulties when it comes to putting into practice the sustainable business strategy that we wish for.

7.10 | | Ring by Adoro mi oro
Ring from the Bishnoi collection made from 18k Fairmined gold, champagne diamond, rose-cut brown diamond, blue diamond and turquoise.
Photo: Ilaria Mauro

7.11 | Ring by Emilie Bliguet
One-off piece made from 18k Fairmined gold.
Photo: Ilaria Mauro

In many cases, and with the objective of overcoming these challenges in a simpler and more affordable way, these adversities end up producing key partnerships that involve sharing the burden in terms of management, suppliers and production runs.

The Oh My Gold collective comprises three designers of different nationalities. From their base in Barcelona, they share a passion for conscious consumption and a clear idea of what sustainable luxury represents.

Adriana Díaz, Emilie Bliguet and Katja Jesek (with her firm Adoro mi Oro) work independently on creating and designing their own collections, but what they have in common is their use of Fairmined metals and conflict-free diamonds from Australia. This has given them the opportunity to form a partnership to obtain these materials more easily than if they tried to do so alone.

7.12 | Pendant by Adriana Díaz
Pendant from the Laur collection made from Fairmined .925 silver.
Photo: Adriana Díaz

This coincidence of common objectives makes it easier to acquire certifications, allows savings on various ensuing costs and lowers the technical hurdles that metalsmiths encounter fairly frequently when producing a piece.

Oh My Gold also aims to teach consumers about the concept of ethical jewellery, and it additionally offers its knowledge and experience to help jewellery makers who are looking to establish a jewellery firm with ethical values.

Communicating with consumers

Communicating and sharing are part of any commercial strategy for a product. All jewellery firms undertake communications activities to reach consumers and convey the values and essence that make them different from everyone else.

When a designer or firm incorporates sustainability as one of the key pillars of its values and philosophy, it is necessary to tell consumers about it so that they interpret this distinctiveness as added value.

As has previously been said, elements linked to the product such as catalogues, websites or packaging can convey— whether through their materials, colour or design—that the firm has opted for sustainability in all of its processes. It is important for consumers to recognize that the jewellery pieces are different and worth their being won over by them. To achieve this, it is necessary to use all the tools that we have access to.

7.13 | Ring by the firm Fair Trade Jewellery Co., made from recycled 18k pink gold and marquise-cut diamond produced in a laboratory

This Canadian firm communicates with consumers so that they have a full understanding of what it means for a jewellery piece to be sustainable. Its packaging and photographic style as well as all the information available on its website offer a clear example of how to communicate exceptional values such as sustainability and ethical responsibility.

Photo: Kathleen Kerr/FTJCo.

When we put out external communications, that should not be limited to the firm's own channels. It is helpful to address specialist online outlets that cover fashion and accessories related to sustainability, with the goal of highlighting our presence as a brand with ethical values. Many of these channels are blogs that are eager to share new offerings with their readers and followers, who are part of the group of aware consumers that opts for ethics when buying a product.

Educating consumers

Because the jewellery sector is by its nature secretive, revealing to the general public the origin of the most frequently used raw materials in jewellery when we talk about social practices or the industry's impact on the environment is a complicated task.

For this reason, it is absolutely necessary for consumers to understand the way in which conventional jewellery harms the planet. The intricacies of the problem must be explained in a clear and simple way so that everything can be easily assimilated. Too much information can cause confusion and even a certain level of rejection.

FASHION ME GREEN

7.14 | Fashion Me Green Blog

Greta Eagan is an American blogger who specializes in sustainable fashion and style. Her Fashion Me Green blog gives exposure to fashion firms and accessories and jewellery brands that have sustainable and ethical practices at their core. Firms such as Odette New York and Rêve En Vert have been written about in some of the site's posts.
www.fashionmegreen.com

Photo: Felicia Lasala

Awareness-raising campaigns and activities

One way to make consumers reflect on the responsibility that we all share when it comes to buying products is campaigns or activities that raise awareness about a specific problem.

This point is demonstrated by Tiffany & Co. and its #KnotOnMyPlanet campaign. The objective of the initiative is to raise funds for the fight against elephant poaching and to halt the trade in and global demand for ivory.

The firm exhibits a clear commitment to sustainability in many of the activities and campaigns that it promotes, and this reaches consumers.

The Tiffany & Co. Foundation also offers support to organizations that manage natural resources in the areas of responsible mining, coral conservation and urban parks. Specifically, the foundation promotes responsible mining through land preservation and rehabilitation as well as efforts to establish standards; conservation of coral through key research and specific educational outreach; and the improvement of urban parks through beautification and infrastructural improvements.

7.15 | Elephant Schlumberger® brooch made from 18k yellow gold and platinum with diamonds, coloured gems and Pallioné enamel by Tiffany & Co.

This piece, which belongs to Tiffany & Co.'s Masterpieces 2016 collection, was used in the #KnotOnMyPlanet campaign, the aim of which is to condemn elephant poaching and raise awareness about the effects of the ivory trade.

Photo: Tiffany & Co.

7.16 | The model Doutzen Kroes sporting a knot in her top as part of the #KnotOnMyPlanet campaign

The objective of Tiffany & Co.'s #KnotOnMyPlanet campaign is to collect donations for the Elephant Crisis Fund to combat elephant poaching. It received support on social networks from many international models, including Doutzen Kroes, Imaan Hammam, Constance Jablonski and Fernanda Ly.

Photo: Dan Jackson

Styling: Alastair McKimm

Collaborations

Collaborations with certain entities or organizations represent a good opportunity to connect with consumers, and since the issue here is sustainability, actions of this type are a way of raising awareness about both the need to create jewellery that is more environmentally respectful and fair trade.

In 2011, British designer Anna Loucah created a series of jewellery pieces within the Green Carpet Challenge, an initiative by Livia Firth involving the collaboration of Vogue magazine. The challenge was to promote sustainable and ethical fashion, giving it exposure through moments on the red carpet at international film events.

Anna Loucah's pieces made from ethically sourced raw materials were exhibited at the Golden Globes gala and at the Cannes Film Festival in 2011 by Livia and Colin Firth, which put out the message that making jewellery in an ethical and sustainable way is possible.

7.17 | Radiance ring by designer Anna Loucah

Made from ecological, Fairtrade-certified 18k white gold with ethically sourced diamonds and tourmaline, this piece was part of the Green Carpet Challenge, which was led by Livia Firth and featured the collaboration of Vogue magazine.

Photo: Hanover Saffron

This collaboration was an important step towards sustainability within the jewellery world, since it presented the first international certification for precious metals extracted in an environmentally friendly manner and in accordance with high ethical standards for all those involved in the sector.

Anna Loucah's Juana ring became the first piece of jewellery to be made from Fairmined- and Fairtrade-certified gold, a development that opened up the way for many designers to use the same certifications to guarantee the sustainability of the metals that they use to create their jewellery.

The collaboration ended with a charity auction of jewellery pieces on behalf of Oxfam. A total of 80,000 pounds was raised for good causes.

Nowadays there are various high jewellery firms that take part in the Green Carpet Challenge, and each year they share their new ethical and sustainable collections.

7.18 | Anna Loucah's Juana ring
Made from 18k ecological white gold with Fairtrade and Fairmined certifications and with ethically sourced diamonds and aquamarine, the piece is a historic achievement that has great relevance because of its status as the first jewellery piece in the world to use sustainable gold with these certifications.

Photo: Hanover Saffron

Chopard

7.19

7.20

In 2013, Swiss high jewellery firm Chopard, alongside Eco-Age, a sustainability-strategies consultancy that was founded by its creative director Livia Firth, joined forces to create a programme called The Journey, with the shared goal of laying the foundations for sustainable luxury.

7.19 | Earrings from the Green Carpet collection by Chopard

Laurel branch earrings from the Green Carpet collection made from 18k Fairmined-certified ethical white gold with marquise-cut diamonds supplied by a certified member of the Responsible Jewellery Council.

Photo: © Chopard & Cie.

7.20 | A Chopard craftsperson setting princess-cut diamonds

A Chopard craftsperson using a burin as part of an artisanal setting technique to make one of the earring sets in the Green Carpet collection.

Photo: © Chopard & Cie.

This initiative led to cooperation between Chopard and the Alliance for Responsible Mining. The fruit of this relationship was Chopard's Green Carpet high jewellery collection, which is made from sustainable Fairmined gold and diamonds from suppliers certified by the Responsible Jewellery Council. The collection was presented at the Cannes Film Festival in 2013.

Thanks also to its collaboration with various international actresses such as Cate Blanchett, who was wearing a pair of its earrings when she won the Best Actress award at the 2014 Golden Globes, Chopard has managed to ignite great interest across the media regarding what the luxury sector should look like now and in the future in terms of ethical practices. It also serves as an example to both high jewellery firms and end consumers.

Chopard and the Cannes Film Festival are an example of how to promote sustainable development in the luxury sector.

Following the rewarding experience of creating the Green Carpet high jewellery collection, in 2014 Chopard took another step forward by using Fairmined-certified gold to make the Palme d'Or, the award that is handed out each year for the best film at the Cannes Film Festival and that was redesigned by the firm in 1998. This undoubtedly introduced sustainable luxury jewellery on the international scene.

7.21

Since then, Chopard has worked with clear objectives to continue its sustainability journey. It has created new partnerships and initiatives so that the raw materials selected comply with strict transparency requirements that guarantee their ethical origins and support for local communities.

7.21 | Rings from the Ice Cube collection by Chopard

Outside the Green Carpet high jewellery collection, Chopard has also opted for the use of Fairmined-certified sustainable gold in its Ice Cube collection.

Photo: © Chopard & Cie.

7.22 | Palme d'Or from the Cannes International Film Festival

The award is produced from ethical, Fairmined-certified gold held in crystal shaped as an emerald-cut diamond.

Photo: © Chopard & Cie.

Joan Gomis

7.23

7.24

The founding of Misui was driven by the sixth generation of the Vendrell family, the founders of Unión Suiza. Misui was set up with the aim of rethinking the idea of luxury in the twenty-first century and adopting values linked to respect for the environment, the sector, the craft, its talent and its people. Director Joan Gomis explains his ethical engagement.

7.23 | Joan Gomis
Director of Misui.
Photo: Cristina Gomis

7.24 |Ring Klar of the collection One of a Kind by Misui
Designed by Marc Monzó and made from 18k Fairmined gold. Gems: Heliodor, spessartine and Spirit®-cut diamond.
Photo: Cristina Gomis

When did Misui decide to work with Fairmined metals?

From the beginning, prior to creating the brand, we felt that we should integrate the values of respect for the environment and people into all of our processes. It is difficult in a twenty-first-century society to view luxury as something that does not contemplate this awareness present among a significant part of society. Likewise, another value that we consider to be fundamental is acknowledging and communicating the authorship of the jewellers and craftspeople who contribute their creativity to make Misui a contemporary jewellery brand.

7.25 | Ring Klar of the collection One of a Kind by Misui
Klar Ooak ring designed by Estela Guitart and made from 18k Fairmained gold, with tourmaline, aquamarine and golden beryl.
Photo: Cristina Gomis

How does that factor have an impact during the jewellery-production phase?

It depends on whether we are talking about one-off or collection pieces. In the first case, Fairmined gold presents no difference relative to other types of gold. With regard to the second, fitting collection pieces into production processes is more complex and requires significant investment. At Misui, when the initial processes for obtaining plate or thread make the use of Fairmined gold impossible, we use the London Bullion Market Association's "Responsible Gold Certificate" gold—that is, recycled gold—and we communicate this on the authenticity certificate.

7.26 | One of a Kind ring by Misui
Designed by Estela Guitart and made from 18k Fairmined gold with tourmaline, beryl and blue-grey tourmaline cut by Munsteiner.
Photo: Cristina Gomis

7.25

Joan Gomis

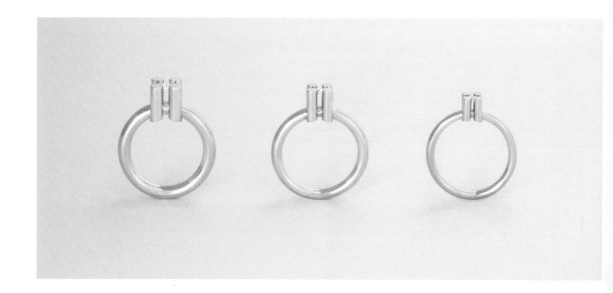

What role does "new luxury" sustainability play at Misui and in the rest of the jewellery industry?

We don't conceive of the possibility of generating beauty when it has negative consequences on the environment and people. In our view, it would be a contradiction that we make sure to avoid.

Misui collaborates with designers such as Marc Monzó, Estela Guitart and Noon Passama. What was the experience of working with sustainable raw materials like for them?

In fact, Marc, Estela, Noon and Marta Boan—Misui's most recent incorporation—are people who share these values, and as a result the process is absolutely natural, and it couldn't be otherwise. They feel good about it and are delighted, as our customers are.

7.27 | Solitaire rings from the Bridal collection by Misui

Ring designed by Marc Monzó and made from 18k Fairmined yellow gold and diamonds.

Photo: Cristina Gomis

What advice would you give to new designers who want to make their collections environmentally responsible and ethical?

I don't like to give advice. In any case, I would ask that the decisions taken by both designers and the industry, as well as their practices, are as rigorous as their communication activities are, since otherwise they would become mere pseudo-marketing activities with negative consequences.

Not all societies have the same level of environmental awareness, but as this awareness increases, I think that the sector will have to adopt it generally.

What is your view on the place that sustainable practices will have at different jewellery firms in the future?

The truth is that I can't predict the future. I would like them to become more widespread, and I think that they will, but it will depend on decisions that we can only hope to influence.

7.28 | Ring from the Klar collection by Misui

Top view of a Klar Ooak ring designed by Estela Guitart in 18k Fairmined gold, with golden beryl and tourmalines.

Photo: Cristina Gomis

7.29 | Third Spirit ring by Misui

Third Spirit ring designed by Marc Monzó in 18k Fairmined gold, with morganite, aquamarine and diamond.

Photo: Cristina Gomis

Having reached this point in the book, it is necessary to finish off by reflecting on the benefits of launching a jewellery firm in a sustainable manner and the responsibilities that we have within the supply chain.

Reward

Launching a sustainable jewellery project requires a series of indisputable efforts, as we have seen throughout this book. However, due to the nature of the problem that we are seeking to solve, those efforts also produce both personal and professional satisfaction of a kind that is difficult to describe, and this satisfaction is strengthened by the security of knowing that we are contributing to the general good.

Moreover, there are also business advantages and results that can be obtained in the long run.
First of all, the sustainable business option opens up the possibility of accessing new markets that would otherwise be out of our reach.

7.30

If we know how to position our brand correctly, we can establish customer loyalty as a result of the added value offered by our jewellery. This will likely help us to significantly increase sales.

Another positive aspect is that the product's added value will also by extension be gained by the brand, which will be a positive when it comes to seeking grants or tendering.

7.31 | Pendant from the Core Gold collection by Tejen made from 18k Fairmined gold with a conflict-free diamond

Isabel Encinias and Mark Kroeker are the founders of Tejen, a firm that offers environmentally aware luxury products.
The firm has successfully managed to position itself without the concept of sustainability having been an impediment of any kind to its growth.

Photo: Terry Gates

7.30 | Gold Arc earrings from the Core Gold collection by Tejen made from 18k Fairmined gold

Photo: Dimitri Tolstoï

7.31

The circle of responsibilities

To understand what responsibilities each of us has and achieve success in undertaking sustainable practices, it is necessary to understand the responsibilities of the rest of the elements of the chain in allowing jewellery to be made and sold.

Illegal mining, large mining corporations, distributors, suppliers, designers and jewellery firms are all part of the chain leading up to where the jewellery reaches the consumer. And each of them has the responsibility to contribute to transforming the industry.

The fragility of the chain hinges upon the precarity experienced by many of the elements involved; we should not forget that jewellery and the producing or obtaining of its raw materials mobilizes a high level of capital each year, which means that often people look the other way when it comes to choosing ethical values.

Mining

Depending on the country and individuals' circumstances, people who work in illegal mining normally have no other form of subsistence, and so they will do anything to get by, without their taking into account the industry's impact on the environment. This is understandable when particular communities don't have the information or resources to carry out their activities in a more sustainable way.

In these cases, responsibility must fall upon countries' governments so that they offer solutions that guarantee everyone's well-being and control improper activities in order to make sure that resource extraction is carried out without damaging the environment or communities. There are many training projects and organizations—for example, the Artisanal Gold Council and the Alliance for Responsible Mining—that do great work, but they require support from governments and even international bodies such as the UN.

The large-scale mining industry should commit to studying the impact that each mine might have, and it should create completely transparent programmes to guarantee stability through social actions and offsetting.

7.32 | Miner in La Llanada, Colombia, working in a mine under ARM standards

The Alliance for Responsible Mining's objective is for small-scale mining operations to carry out their activities in a formal, organized and profitable manner and to use efficient technologies so as to be socially and environmentally responsible.

Photo: Manuela Franco

Suppliers

Until this point, we have been talking about the start of the supply chain, which is characterized by vulnerability due to its social characteristics. However, each distributor or provider is also responsible for the origins and extraction methods of the raw materials that it wishes to trade in, as depending on its ethical involvement, it can contribute to upsetting the fragility of the previous link in the chain.

For this reason, it is important to prioritize suppliers and distributors that offer complete transparency, whether they work with metals or gems. Doing so will provide solutions to the root of the problem.

Designers and firms

It is necessary for jewellery firms and designers to understand the root of the problem, since this is essential in order to demand total transparency from distributors, even if doing so goes against the secrecy and silence that have always characterized this sector. In this case, the designer's responsibilities are to become sufficiently informed so as to obtain raw materials of ethical origins and establish the partnerships necessary for any production process.

Using creativity in pursuit of new sustainable solutions through innovation and a demand for ethical and sustainable raw materials can also make suppliers reconsider how they conduct their various activities, reducing the impact that they had had until that moment.

The designer or the firm therefore has the role of educating customers and making them aware through the channels available.

Consumers

The current level of development allows consumers to have access to a very large quantity of information on any Internet-connected device in just a click. We might say that it has never been as easy to learn about any subject as it is now. As consumers, our responsibility is to ask ourselves about the origins of the products that we consume, whether they be coffee, clothing or jewellery. We have to back products that have been ethically made or obtained and that meet guarantees that are sufficiently transparent so as to deserve our trust. If there is no awareness to our consumption, all the previous links in the chain will stop fulfilling their missions and objectives.

7.33 | Circle of responsibilities in the jewellery-creation cycle

Sharing ethical responsibilities among all parts of the chain will facilitate sustainable practices in the jewellery sector.

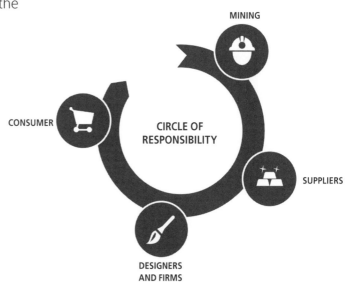

CONSUMER

MINING

CIRCLE OF RESPONSIBILITY

SUPPLIERS

DESIGNERS AND FIRMS

Present and future

The jewellery sector as it is today very clearly tells us about what its future will be like. We can see that there are more and more firms that use raw materials from fair mining, motivated by a personal ethical philosophy that reasserts the right meaning that the luxury sector deserves.

But when it is the large, internationally known firms that are incorporating these practices, the conclusion is that sustainability in the jewellery world is something that will be decisive in the future and that the longer it takes for firms or designers to adopt sustainable strategies, the more difficult it will be for them to get ahead in the market.

Many organizations are doing exceptional work to turn the jewellery sector into an ethical industry at all levels, and through the support of small and large firms and creators, once-modest projects such as Green Gold have turned into a reality and a necessity.

There is undoubtedly still a long road ahead, but through innovative initiatives and the new talents that the future has in store, sustainability will continue to open up the way to offering a decent life to many people who currently do not have one, and it will awaken a general sense of love for the environment and a respectful use of resources that belong to all of us.

7.34 | Nobel Peace Prize medal made by Norwegian company Samlerhuset with Fairmined-certified gold

Since 2015, and in collaboration with the Alliance for Responsible Mining, Samlerhuset has made the Nobel Peace Prize medal with Fairmined-certified gold, backing a form of small-scale mining that means opportunities and sustainable development.

Photo: © Samlerhuset Group B.V.

Adoro mi oro
www.adoromioro.com

Adriana Díaz
www.adrianadiazh.com

Amanda Li Hope
www.amandalihope.com

Ana González
www.anagonzalezjoyas.com

Anna Loucah
www.annaloucah.com

ARM
www.responsiblemines.org

Artisanal Gold Council
www.artisanalgold.org

Bario Neal
bario-neal.com

Chopard
www.chopard.com

Eco-Age
eco-age.com

Elephant Crisis Fund
savetheelephants.org

Emilie Bliguet
www.emiliebliguetethicaljewellery.com

Fair Trade Jewellery Co.
ftjco.com

Fairtrade Gold
www.fairgold.org

Fashion Me Green
www.fashionmegreen.com

Fluid Jewellery
www.fluidjewellery.com

Goldfingers
goldfingers.dk

Green Carpet Challenge
eco-age.com/green-carpet-challenge

#knotonmyplanet
www.knotonmyplanet.org

Misui
www.misui.es

United Nations
www.un.org

Samlerhuset
samlerhuset.com

Sissai
sissai.com

Tejen
tejen-collection.com

Tiffany & Co.
www.tiffany.com

Tiffany & . Foundation
www.tiffanyandcofoundation.org

Tura Sugden
www.turasugden.com

AFTERWORD

The current reality that lies beneath the jewellery industry is a business model in which consumption reflects constant growth that pays no attention to the damaging impact that it leaves behind. We can see this reality is widespread in many sectors, where what comes first is having a lot of everything as soon as possible.

The positive dimension of this is that such situations have raised a collective awareness that we can see among many designers, firms and consumers. It is a change of perceptions that will surely become stronger and promote consumption based on empathy and the human quality behind every jewellery piece.

The renewed appreciation of craftsmanship, handmade pieces and local production are all indicators of this new kind of market, which seeks to offer goods removed from mass production and globalization. Instead, it provides products that have been lovingly made by their creators and customized for people who want their consumption to be intelligent. But if we reflect and ask the right questions, we will discover that this change is not the end of the discussion and that, if we do not establish a sustainable strategy that takes the entire supply chain into account, the consequences of our activities will completely run counter to our wishes.

Taking the path towards sustainability mainly requires us to be curious and to ask ourselves where things come from and if we can do things in a better way. To this end, we need to make creative efforts and personally back the creation of a new blueprint in which sustainability plays a part from start to finish. This will be essential if we are to reach a market that offers us new, forward-looking opportunities.

I hope that in this book you have found all the help needed to work in a sustainable way. The next step is to continue researching by visiting the links to the different associations, organizations, certifications and suppliers that are available among the resources in this book. Analysing the steps taken by the firms and designers presented here will make it easier for you to establish a realistic strategy that is based on your needs and the features of your business.

I also hope that reading this work has given you the motivation needed to take the path towards change.

Firms and designers

Adoro mi oro

Spain
www.adoromioro.com

Adriana Díaz

Spain
www.adrianadiazh.com

Amalena

Austria
www.amalena.es

Amanda Li Hope

United Kingdom
www.amandalihope.com

Ana González

Colombia
www.anagonzalezjoyas.com

Ana Khouri

United States
www.anakhouri.com

Anna Loucah

United Kingdom
www.annaloucah.com

Anna Moltke-Huitfeldt

Denmark
www.moltke-huitfeldt.com

April Doubleday

United Kingdom
www.aprildoubleday.com

Arabel Lebrusan

United Kingdom
www.arabellebrusan.com

Article 22

United States
www.article22.com

As Above So Below

United States
asabove8sobelow.com

Atty Tantivit

Thailand
www.attagallery.com

Bario Neal

United States
bario-neal.com

Camilla Pietropaoli

Italy
www. camillapi.com

Cherry Boonyapan

Thailand
www.cherryboonyapan.com

Chopard

Switzerland
www.chopard.com

Coral Covey

Germany
coralcovey.com

Diamond Foundry

United States
www.diamondfoundry.com

Edun

United States
edun.com

Elena Estaun

Spain
www.elenaestaun.com

Emilie Bliguet

Spain
emiliebliguetethicaljewellery.com

Epaulettes

Spain
www.epaulettes.es

Fair Trade Jewellery Co.

Canada
www.ftjco.com

Fluid Jewellery

Canada
www.fluidjewellery.com

Goldfingers

Denmark
goldfingers.dk

Jaume Labro

Japan
www.jaumelabro.com

JEM

France
www.jem-paris.com

Kamoka Pearls

United States
kamokapearls.com

Firms and designers

Kata Sangkhae

Thailand
www.katasangkhae.com

Koetania

Spain
www.koetania.com

Lia Terni

Spain
www.liaterni.com

Louis Vuitton

France
www. louisvuitton.com

Made

United Kingdom
www.made.uk.com

Majoral

Spain
www.majoral.com

Maral Rapp

United States
www.maralrapp.com

María Goti

Spain
www.mariagoti.es

Marta Blanco

Spain
www.marutadas.com

Martalia

Ecuador
www.martalia.com

Melville Fine Jewellery

Hong Kong
www.melvillejewellery.com

Misui

Spain
www.misui.es

Nanini

Netherlands
www.nanini.nl

Nehcaa

Spain
nehcaajewelry.com

Riviera Rebel

United Kingdom
rivierarebel.co.uk

SeeMe

Netherlands
www.seeme.org

Sissai

Peru
sissai.com

Soko

United States
www.shopsoko.com

Tejen

United States
tejen-collection.com

The Rock Hound

United Kingdom
www.therockhound.com

Tiffany & Co.

United States
www.tiffany.com

Toby Pomeroy

United States
www.tobypomeroy.com

Tura Sugden

United States
www.turasugden.com

Ute Decker

United Kingdom
www.utedecker.com

VK Designs

United States
www.valkasinskas.com

Suppliers

A&E Metals
Recycled metals in different formats.

Australia
www.aemetal.com.au

Ananas Anam
Sustainable plant-based fabrics.

United Kingdom
www.ananas-anam.com

Columbia Gem House
Natural and ethically sourced coloured gems.

Canada
www.columbiagemhouse.com

Cookson Gold
Recycled metals and Fairtrade gold in different formats.

Spain - United Kingdom
www.cooksongold.es

Diamond Foundry
Laboratory-made diamonds.

United States
www.diamondfoundry.com

Gemfields
Natural and ethically sourced coloured gems.

United Kingdom
www.gemfields.co.uk

Hoover & Strong
Recycled metals in different formats.

United States
www.hooverandstrong.com

Kamoka Pearls
Sustainable plant-based fabrics.

United States
kamokapearls.com

Niccolò Bella
Ethically sourced coloured gems and diamonds.

United States
www.niccolobella.com

neteen 48
Ethically sourced coloured gems and diamonds.

United Kingdom
www.nineteen48.com

Origin Australia
Ethically sourced coloured gems and diamonds.

Australia
www.originaustralia.com

Pure Grown Diamonds
Laboratory-made diamonds.

United States
www.puregrowndiamonds.com

Ruby Fair
Ethically sourced coloured gems and rubies.

United Kingdom
www.rubyfair.com

Self Packaging
Sustainable packaging.

Spain
www.selfpackaging.com

Stuller
Recycled metals in different formats.

United States
www.stuller.com

Sugar Artists' Acrylic
Ecological spray paints.

Australia
sugarartistsacrylic.com

Tiny Box Company
Sustainable packaging.

United Kingdom
www.tinyboxcompany.co.uk

Umicore
Recycled metals.

Belgium
www.umicore.com

United Precious Metals
Recycled metals in different formats.

United States
www.unitedpmr.com

Vipa Design
Microfusion with Fairtrade, Fairmined and recycled metals.

United Kingdom
www.vipadesigns.co.uk

Certifications

CanadaMark
Certification for ethically sourced diamonds from Canada.

Canada
www.canadamark.com

Fairmined
Sustainability and fair trade certification for metals such as gold, silver and platinum.

Colombia
www.fairmined.org

Fairtrade
Sustainability and fair trade certification for metals such as gold, silver and platinum.

United Kingdom
www.fairgold.org

SCS Global Services
Standard certification for sustainable products.

United States
www.scsglobalservices.com

Rapaport Fair Trade
Independent certification for fair-trade diamonds and precious stones.

United States
www.rapaportfairtrade.com

Organizations

Alliance for Responsible Mining
Independent organization that promotes responsibility standards and criteria for small-scale and artisanal mining.

Colombia
www.responsiblemines.org

Artisanal Gold Council
Organization devoted to improving the opportunities, environment and health of the millions of people involved in artisanal gold mining.

Canada
www.artisanalgold.org

Ethical Metalsmiths
Organization dedicated to fostering ethical and sustainable practices in jewellery.

United States
www.ethicalmetalsmiths.org

Fair Jewelry Action
Platform for fostering ethical and sustainable practices in jewellery.

United Kingdom
www.fairjewelry.org

Global Witness
Environmental and human rights NGO.

United Kingdom
www.globalwitness.org

Joyería Sostenible
Platform dedicated to fostering ethical and sustainable practices in jewellery design.

Spain
www.joyeriasostenible.com

No Dirty Gold
International campaign working to ensure that gold mining operations respect the environment and human rights.

United States
nodirtygold.earthworksaction.org

Responsible Jewellery Council
International organization that ensures transparency in the jewellery industry's supply chain.

United Kingdom
www.responsiblejewellery.com

Sustainable Pearls
Platform for fostering ethical and sustainable practices in jewellery.

United States
www.sustainablepearls.org

The Jeweltree Foundation

Foundation focused on sustainable development and fair trade in precious metals, coloured gems and diamonds.

Netherlands
www.jeweltreefoundation.org

Tiffany & Co. Foundation

Foundation offering support to organizations focused on protecting resources in the areas of responsible mining and coral protection.

United States
tiffanyandcofoundation.org

Acknowledgements

First of all, I would like to thank the whole Promopress team, and especially Montse Borràs and Joaquim Canet for supporting my idea for the book and giving me this opportunity.

I would like to thank all the brands, communications agencies, authors and designers for their involvement in the book. It has been a privilege to be able to turn to their experience, and truly moving to feel the enthusiasm that they have shown towards the project.

I am thankful to Cherry Booyapan, with whom I have shared the whole creative process. This project would have been impossible without her coordinating work.

I am grateful to Johanna Mejía and Jaume Labro for generously sharing their great knowledge and friendship.

I would like to thank Greg Valerio for contributing his experienced take on sustainability in the book's foreword.

I give thanks also to all the teams at Fairmined and ARM, and in particular to Conny Havel, who was always willing to help me, for her great kindness and professionalism.

I would additionally like to pay special tribute to the photographers Mauricio Vélez, Manuela Franco and Malú Cabellos. Through their fantastic photos, they have provided the touch of humanity that the book needed.

Lastly, I wish to thank Jose Luis and Silvana for their unconditional support.